WHERE WAS GOD?

ANSWERS TO TOUGH QUESTIONS
ABOUT GOD AND NATURAL DISASTERS

WHERE WAS GOD?

ANSWERS TO TOUGH QUESTIONS ABOUT GOD AND NATURAL DISASTERS

ERWIN W. LUTZER

Tyndale House Publishers, Inc. Carol Stream, Illinois

Visit Tyndale's exciting Web site at www.tyndale.com

TYNDALE and Tyndale's quill logo are registered trademarks of Tyndale House Publishers, Inc.

Where Was God? Answers to tough questions about God and natural disasters

Designed by Jennifer Ghionzoli

Library of Congress Cataloging-in-Publication Data

Lutzer, Erwin W.
   Where was God? : answers to tough questions about God and natural disasters / Erwin W. Lutzer.
      p. cm.
   Includes bibliographical references.
   ISBN-13: 978-1-4143-1144-9 (hc)
   ISBN-10: 1-4143-1144-3 (hc)
   1. Disasters—Religious aspects—Christianity. 2. Providence and government of God. 3. God—Omnipresence. I. Title.
   BT161.L88 2006
   231'.8—dc22   2006016064

Printed in the United States of America

11   10   09   08   07   06
7   6   5   4   3   2   1

For R. C. Sproul, a friend who never tires of reminding us that God is sovereign both in history and in nature, and that our trust in Him is well placed.

God is our refuge and strength,
an ever-present help in trouble.
Therefore we will not fear, though the earth give way
and the mountains fall into the heart of the sea,
though its waters roar and foam
and the mountains quake with their surging. . . .
"Be still, and know that I am God;
I will be exalted among the nations,
I will be exalted in the earth."
The LORD Almighty is with us;
the God of Jacob is our fortress.

PSALM 46:1-3, 10-11

CONTENTS

A HEART FOR THE HURTING

This book was birthed in my heart while I was watching a CNN special report on the children who survived the deadly October 8, 2005, earthquake in India and Pakistan. As I watched volunteers trying to help the frightened youngsters, the question that came to my mind was, "What kind of a God would allow such a disaster to happen?"

These children—most of them orphaned—were bandaged and bruised. Some had eyes swollen shut, while others sat in stoney silence, evidently in shock at what they had experienced. Now without adequate facilities, volunteers were doing what they could to provide comfort and the basic necessities to the survivors. But many people trapped in remote villages had no help whatsoever.

Without a doubt, many of those children have already died since the CNN special was aired, and those who survived face a life of loneliness, heartache, and pain. In all, eighty thousand people died in the 2005 quake and many times that number sustained injuries.

This earthquake came right on the heels of the largest natural disaster in modern history, the tsunami that swept through Sri Lanka, Thailand, India, and a number of other countries in December 2004. The estimated death toll following that disaster is now at 240,000, although no one knows for sure.

As I write this, one year after the tsunami, 2 million people are still homeless and many of them have hardly even begun to put their lives back together. Children are still struggling, families are fragmented, and fifty thousand people are listed as missing. Even today, some people are still searching for a child or relative, hoping against hope that they will yet be found alive. Who can calculate the buckets of tears wept because of disasters like this?

Those of us who live in the United States immediately think of Hurricane Katrina, which washed away much of the Gulf Coast in August 2005. Pictures of the thousands of people gathering aimlessly around the Superdome are etched in our minds. The stories are legion: A mother calls to her child as he is swept away in the rising waters. A family huddled in their attic wave frantically for rescuers, hoping they will be spared. In all, more than one thousand people died, and hundreds of thousands were left behind to try to regain some kind of normalcy. Survivors tell of fighting for insurance payments and living in shelters, knowing that their homes can never be rebuilt. And in the wake of this disaster, many children are still missing.

In all, the 2005 hurricane season was the most active in history: Twenty-seven tropical storms (including fourteen hurricanes) were named. But the devastation in lesser-known disasters is just as terrible for individual families and children. Tragedies on a smaller scale kill and destroy every day, though only the large-scale events make the news.

Some people think we should not seek answers from God or from man. They believe that these disasters are of such gigantic proportions that there cannot possibly be any hidden meaning in them, nor can anything helpful or encouraging be said about them.

I am well aware that little or nothing can be said to ease the pain of those who mourn the loss of loved ones. Parents will hardly be comforted when a Christian tells them that God has some hidden purpose in the loss of their child. A child who has just learned that his parents died in the collapsed house behind him would not be comforted by the assurance that God really does care and that He did this for some better end.

Glib answers can be hurtful, not helpful. Sometimes we just need to sit beside those who grieve, letting them know we care rather than talking to them dispassionately about God's promises and purposes. I've found that it's often better to say nothing than to say something that appears to trivialize the horror. There is a grief that is too deep for words, too deep for explanations, and yes, even too deep for human comfort.

How well I recall the words of Fyodor Dostoyevsky as he

vividly describes the sufferings of small children and wonders about the problem of evil in *The Brothers Karamazov*: "Imagine you are creating a fabric of human destiny with the object of making men happy in the end, giving them peace and rest at last, but that it was essential and inevitable to torture to death only one tiny creature . . . would you consent to be the architect on those conditions?"[1] The famous writer concludes that such torment can never be justified, that no explanation has ever been developed that can sufficiently answer or explain it. The same can be said about the suffering of children in light of natural evils; the suffering is of such magnitude that it seems futile to believe it can ever be justified. Better to simply give no answer than to give an inadequate one.

Keep in mind that although we use the term *natural evil*, we must make a distinction between natural disasters and the evils men do, which can be traced back to choices made by human beings. A tsunami in the middle of an ocean that did not affect us would not be thought of as evil in and of itself; we speak of it as evil only when we see the devastation it brings to the people who share this planet. It becomes evil because we regard suffering and death as evil.

Despite this clarification, however, we need to ask whether the horrific events we have witnessed are compatible with the God who has revealed Himself in the Bible. Natural disasters challenge the limits of our faith in a good and caring God. How can we watch the news coverage of orphaned children and have our faith still remain intact? Centuries ago, Asaph, who wrote many of the Psalms, found his faith slipping when he saw the wicked prosper and the righteous brought low. He begins with an optimistic statement and then reveals his doubts.

> Surely God is good to Israel, to those who are pure in heart. But as for me, my feet had almost slipped; I had nearly lost my foothold. For I envied the arrogant when I saw the prosperity of the wicked. **PSALM 73:1-3**

Asaph's problem was not a natural disaster, but even so, he found it difficult to reconcile the existence of a good, all-powerful God with the continuing injustice of the world. Who of us has not wondered at the seeming indifference of God toward this planet with its woes, its injustices, and its suffering? In the face of indescribable human grief, God's silence is deafening.

One newsman, commenting on Hurricane Katrina, spoke for many when he said, "If this world is the product of intelligent design, then the designer has some explaining to do." Of course many of us believe that the Designer does *not* owe us an explanation—yet if we believe He has revealed Himself through the Scriptures, we are permitted to have some insight into His ways and purposes in the world.

I have very little to say to those who have angrily made up their minds against the Almighty—except to make this point: When atheists ask why God would permit these evils, they are actually assuming the existence of God even as they rail against Him. If God did not exist, we could not call anything evil, whether the convulsions of nature or the criminal acts of human beings. In an impersonal atheistic world, whatever is, just *is*. No moral judgments are possible. We shall return to this point later in this book.

Ultimately, we are faced with a question of faith. Those who know God will believe He has a justifiable reason for human tragedy, while others will treat such faith with contempt.

I have written this book with several goals in mind.

First, we should find out what the Bible has to say about the relationship between God and natural disasters. Such a study can either turn people away from God (as we shall see, this is what happened to Voltaire) or it can cause us to worship Him with even more focus and awe. In the end, my goal is to provide assurance that the God of the Bible can be trusted, that His promises to those who believe are worthy of our faith and the basis of our hope.

We'll be answering questions such as:

- Should natural disasters be called an act of God?
- Is God's involvement in such tragedies direct or remote?
- Why should we believe that God is even interested in what happens in His world?
- Did people in the Bible experience disasters? And if so, did they continue to believe?

What it comes down to is this: In light of the suffering that seems so unnecessary in this world, do we still trust God with confidence? Is it even possible to trust a God who allows a disaster that He surely could have kept from happening? Or even more to the point, a disaster for which He takes responsibility?

My intention is not to pry into God's diary and pretend that I can see all of His purposes; indeed, there are plenty of His purposes in these disasters that will never be known to us. Ultimately, only God knows all the whys and the wherefores. Rather, I want to show that natural evil is not incompatible with a good and caring God. In our study we shall encounter much mystery, but hopefully, also much insight that will guide us even as we grieve over the ills of this world.

A second purpose of this book is to warn against the well-intentioned but foolish interpretations that are frequently offered when disasters come. As I shall point out, people of all faiths, including Christians, are often far too ready to read into these events precisely what they want to see. We must caution against the comments of sincere people who are quite convinced that they are able to discern the particulars of the divine mind.

In clarifying these issues, we'll take a look at the differences between the function of natural disasters in the Old Testament and those of today. If we do not make this necessary distinction, I believe we can be led to make all kinds of judgments about disasters that are invalid, and even harmful.

Finally, I have written this book in an attempt to comfort all who doubt and suffer. While it is true that the best explanations do not immediately comfort those who are struggling with grief, for those who believe in the God of the Bible, a source of strength and comfort can be found, even when answers are hard to come by.

Although the first half of this book (chapters 1–4) deals largely with the more theological and philosophical questions about natural evil, the second half (chapters 5–6) is written with pastoral concerns in mind. There I shall urge readers to seek God in faith and keep believing no matter what tragedies come to this planet. I will also discuss our personal struggles with doubt, and what to say when friends ask us about God and His relationship to the tragedies we see every day on television. The epilogue challenges us to prepare for "The Big One."

For the purposes of this study, I will focus on natural evil rather than evil done by people. Clearly, God does not do the evil perpetuated in a concentration camp; human beings do. But earthquakes and hurricanes cannot be directly connected to decisions made by humans. And, as we shall see, in these tragedies, God's role is more immediate and direct.

Consequently, many Christians who might not lose their faith because of human evil find it more difficult to maintain their faith in the face of natural disasters. Even Christians wonder whether they can trust a God who allows (or causes) such disasters to occur without so much as a single word of comfort from heaven. John Keats wrote, *"Is there another life? Shall I awake and find all this a dream? There must be; we cannot be created for this sort of suffering."*

There can be no doubt that this life will include suffering. But where is God in the face of such pain?

Let us begin our study.

QUESTIONS FOR DISCUSSION

1. Have you or a loved one ever suffered a loss due to natural disaster?

2. In the aftermath of a natural disaster, do you tend to question God's goodness or do you turn to Him for comfort?

3. What passages in the Bible come to mind when thinking of our struggle to believe in God's goodness in difficult times?

CHAPTER 1

DARE WE SEARCH FOR ANSWERS?

God's silence in the presence of human anguish is one of the greatest mysteries of our existence. When faced with gratuitous human suffering, we are forced to rethink our faith, cope with our doubts, and debate whether God can be trusted. When Hurricane Katrina hit the Gulf Coast in August 2005, even those who usually exclude God from their thinking were asking hard questions about human existence as they wrestled with the Divine's apparent indifference to human need.

Just as earthquakes create aftershocks, natural disasters create religious aftershocks that challenge the faith of those who believe in God and simultaneously confirm the cynicism of skeptics. Either way, disasters force us to ask ultimate questions.

The Earthquake That Shook Europe

We begin our discussion, not with contemporary disasters but rather one that dates back to November 1, 1755. The Lisbon earthquake was probably the most far-reaching and

well-known natural disaster in modern history, until the tsunami which occurred late in 2004. Other disasters might
have been worse, but none was so widely discussed or had
such profound ramifications as this one in Portugal.

That morning the sky was bright, calm, and beautiful, but
in a moment everything was transformed into frightening
chaos. Ironically, the earthquake hit on All Saints' Day, when
churches were crowded with worshippers. One would think
that the people who sought shelter in the house of God might
be spared. Indeed, some people even ran into the churches,
seeking shelter by joining the priests who were conducting
mass at 9:30 in the morning. Eyewitnesses say that the crowds
had the terror of death on their faces, and when the second
great shock came, priests and parishioners alike began to
shriek, calling out to God for mercy. But heaven was silent to
their pleas. Almost all of the churches in Lisbon were reduced
to rubble, and the people in them were killed.

After the initial quake, which lasted from six to ten seconds, further aftershocks continued to destroy buildings and
homes. Fire immediately broke out across the city, making
rescue efforts nearly impossible. This havoc was then followed
by a tsunami; its high waves pounded the seaport, tearing
ships from their anchors and drowning hundreds of people
who sought shelter along the coast. The bright morning sky
was darkened with soot and dust. With earth, fire, and water
all combining to increase the destruction, even coolheaded
observers suspected a design.[1]

The earthquake claimed somewhere between thirty and sixty thousand lives, and reduced three-quarters of the city to rubble. Those who remained were forced to rethink many of the important issues of human existence. All throughout Europe there seemed to be a whole new willingness to reopen questions about life beyond the grave, and many people began to talk about building a civilization based on Christianity with its dogged insistence that hope in this life must be rooted in the next. People were faced with the choice of turning against God or believing that He had the power and intention to redeem the evils of this world.

As might be expected, many people clung to their faith, and others sought out faith in Christ for the first time, having been frightfully reminded that their lives were in constant jeopardy. Some historians even say that the age of revolution in France and the age of the Wesleyan revivals in England may have gained impetus from this catastrophe in Portugal.[2] But opinions were by no means unanimous as to how the event should be interpreted. This highlights the difficulty of reading the Divine Mind.

An Interpretation, Please!

The people of Lisbon searched for meaning amid the rubble of destroyed homes and cartloads of dead bodies. Not surprisingly, many believed the earthquake was an act of divine judgment against a sinful seaport city. A famous Jesuit spoke for many when he said, "Learn, O Lisbon, that the destroyers of our houses, palaces, churches and convents, the cause of death of so many people and of the flames that devoured such vast treasures are your abominable sins."[3] After all, the quake came on All Saints' Day, so many assumed God was saying the sins of the saints were so grievous that they merited immediate judgment. What puzzled some, however, was that a street of brothels was left largely intact.

Predictably, Protestants were inclined to say that the earthquake was a judgment against the Jesuits who founded the city. After all, the Inquisition was in full force and tens of thousands of so-called heretics were being brutally murdered. The Jesuits responded by saying that the quake revealed the anger of God because the Inquisition had become too lax.

A Franciscan priest gave his interpretation a twist, arguing that the earthquake was a form of divine mercy. After all, he reasoned, Lisbon deserved much worse: God had every right to destroy the whole city because of its wickedness. Thus he marveled at the restraint of God in allowing some people to live. God graciously did just enough to send a warning and chose to spare some in the city as an act of undeserved mercy so that they could repent.[4]

The parishioners held to the general consensus that this tragedy had to be interpreted in light of a transcendent world. They felt that God was somehow trying to communicate that there is a world beyond this one, a world that can give meaning to the unpredictable and haphazard existence of today. Sermons on the earthquake were preached for years to come.

Whenever tragedy strikes we have a tendency to interpret it in light of what we believe God is trying to say. Back in 2004, some Muslims believed that Allah struck Southeast Asia with a tsunami at Christmastime because the season is so filled with immorality, abomination, alcohol, and the like. And following Katrina, some Muslims opined that Allah was heaping vengeance on the United States for the war in Iraq.

> Whenever tragedy strikes we have a tendency to interpret it in light of what we believe God is trying to say.

On the other hand, a Christian reporter in Israel said that he saw a parallel between the Jewish settlers being forced out of the Gaza Strip and the people being forced out of New Orleans. His implication was that Katrina was a judgment from God for America's support of Israel's decision to vacate parts of the land in favor of the Palestinians. In a further display of supposed divine insight, Pat Robertson suggested that the stroke that ended Ariel Sharon's rule in Israel was God's judgment for having divided "God's land."

There can be little doubt that controversy surrounds the interpretation of natural disasters. This was brought home to me when I was reading the story of John Wycliffe, the great Protestant Bible translator who taught his Oxford University students how to die for the faith. (More than three hundred of his disciples were mercilessly killed for translating and preaching God's Word.)

In 1378, Wycliffe retired from public life to continue his studies and writing at Oxford. In 1381, a peasants' revolt occurred, and one of the leaders of the uprising was John Ball, who had reportedly been a disciple of Wycliffe. Wycliffe disowned the revolt, but the damage was done and he was accused of being an accomplice. Furthermore, the rebels had killed the archbishop of Canterbury, replacing him with William Courtenay, an enemy of Wycliffe.

The following year, the hostile archbishop called a counsel to condemn Wycliffe's statements. When an earthquake came during the proceedings, Wycliffe interpreted it as a sign of divine displeasure, a judgment against those who sought his ousting. Courtenay, however, claimed that the land was breaking wind to expel Wycliffe's foul heresies![5]

Clearly, people see in natural disasters exactly what they want to see. I'm reminded of the remark, "We know that we have created God in our own image when we are convinced that He hates all the same people we do." Disasters often become a mirror in which our own convictions and wishes are reflected.

All of this is a warning that we must be careful about what we say about such tragedies. If we say too much, we may err, thinking we can read the fine print of God's purposes. But if we say nothing, we give the impression that there is no message we can learn from calamities. As we'll see later, I believe that God does speak through these events, but we must be cautious about thinking we know the details of His agenda.

Is This the Best of All Possible Worlds?

Voltaire was living during the Lisbon quake and it affected him deeply. In order to understand his reaction, we have to first be introduced to the philosopher Gottfried von Liebniz, who lived a few decades before the Lisbon quake (1646–1716). He was the first philosopher I know of to write a *theodicy*, a defense of God and His ways in the world.

Think through this bit of philosophical reasoning: Liebniz taught that God had before Him an infinite number of possible worlds, but because God is good, He chose *this* world, which is "the best of all possible worlds," and furthermore, God ordered nature to serve the best of all possible ends. After all, a good God who was sovereign would, of course, do only what was both best and right. Leibniz did not condone evil, but said it must first be a part of a grand scheme, intended for ultimate good. Given the ends He wished to accomplish, this was the best God could do.

Needless to say, after the Lisbon earthquake, people had to ask whether this was indeed "the best of all possible worlds," and if the laws of nature were ordained for the best possible ends. If God was faced with an infinite number of worlds and chose this one, then we rightfully have to ask what the *worst* of all possible worlds would have looked like!

Voltaire was convinced that the Lisbon earthquake put an end to the optimism of those who thought God always acted for the best. Voltaire set out to ridicule the convictions of Christians who believed that there could be some ultimate hidden meaning in the suffering of the world. For him, nothing good could come out of the tragedy at Lisbon, either in this world or the next. He even wrote a poem about the earthquake:

> *"This misery," ye say, "Is others' good."*
> *Yes; from my mouldering body should be born*
> *A thousand worms, when death has closed my pain.*
> *Fine consolation this in my distress! . . .*
> *But how conceive a God supremely good,*
> *Who heaps his favours on the sons he loves*
> *Yet scatters evil with as large a hand? . . .*
> *Tormented atoms in a bed of mud,*
> *Devoured by death, a mockery of fate.*[6]

In a letter to a friend he opined,

> We shall find it difficult to discover how the laws
> of movement operate in such fearful disasters *in*
> *the best of all possible worlds*—where a hundred
> thousand ants, our neighbors, are crushed in a
> second on our ant-heaps, half dying undoubtedly
> in inexpressible agonies, beneath debris from which
> it was impossible to extricate them, families all over
> Europe reduced to beggary, and the fortunes of a
> hundred merchants . . . swallowed up in the ruins
> of Lisbon.[7]

He went on to say that he hoped that the Catholic Inquisitors were crushed like all the others in the quake! He railed against clerics who thought this was a divine judgment on the city. And Voltaire wasn't finished. He went on to write *Candide*, the story of a boy expelled from Paradise who nonetheless believed the world into which he was thrust was "the best of all worlds." With sarcasm and wit, Voltaire describes one tragedy after another, as the boy continues to affirm that it is all for the best.

For example, Candide meets his favorite philosopher, Dr. Pangloss (a follower of Liebniz), who believes that all things happen by necessity and are for the best. After seeing the Lisbon quake, Pangloss says, "All this is for the best; for, if there is a volcano at Lisbon, it cannot be anywhere else; for it is impossible that things should not be where they are; for all is well."[8]

Later in the story, the country's wise men decide that earthquakes can be prevented by burning a few people in a slow fire. So these sages round up a few Jews, along with Candide and his philosopher friend, Dr. Pangloss, and lock them up in prison for a week. They then march through the streets, with miters on their heads bearing strange paintings. Candide is flogged as a hymn is being sung. The Jews are burned and Pangloss is hanged. On the same day, the earth quakes again with a fearful crash.

Candide, terrified, dumbfounded, bewildered, bleeding, and quivering says to himself, "If this is the best of all possible worlds, what are the others? [I could] let it pass that I was flogged . . . but O my dear Pangloss! The greatest of philosophers! Must I see you hanged without knowing why!"[9]

You get the point: As the book progresses, Candide affirms that rape, theft, murder, bankruptcy, and other untold human sufferings must all be optimistically accepted as the best of all possible worlds. With biting sarcasm Voltaire makes a mockery of the notion that God acts for the best, or that He chose the best plan for the world. Voltaire came to the conclusion that evil is unredeemable, that we have no right to discern a higher end to human suffering and tragedy. In this way Voltaire heaped contempt on Christians who believed that surely God had a legitimate purpose in such evils.

We must pause for a moment and ask, *Is this the best of all possible worlds?* If we say yes, the answer seems obviously wrong. Paradise would be the best of all possible worlds, not our world with its suffering, corruption, and endless tragedy.

Looking through our lens, no one could reasonably say this is the best of all possible worlds. If it were, then theoretically, we couldn't improve it. Yet the book of Hebrews uses the word *better* thirteen times, and says that the biblical heroes longed for a "better country—a heavenly one" (Hebrews 11:16), and that God has planned something better for us (see v. 40). Thus we work hard to make things better because we know this is not the best the world can be.

Yet it's difficult to be completely satisfied with such an answer. There is more to this matter than we might initially realize. The Bible does teach that God created all things for His own pleasure and for His own glory. And we read, "In him we were also chosen, having been predestined according to the plan of him who works out everything in conformity with the purpose of his will" (Ephesians 1:11). If all things work to the glory of God, if indeed the details of history—along with human and natural evil—all contribute to His eternal purpose, wouldn't it be accurate to say that this plan is the best, if only we could see it from God's point of view? Does He see our tragedies through a different lens? Might there be a good and wise reason for the madness?

Voltaire was right in saying that from our point of view this is not the best of all possible worlds, but he was wrong in assuming that there could be no hidden purposes in an earthquake. As Christians we believe that God is able to use tragedies for the best of all possible purposes and goals. God has not allowed His creation to spin out of control; He must have a morally sufficient reason that justifies our pain and suffering. So, although we have to look at these disasters through our eyes, we must also view them through the eyes of God as revealed in the Bible. We see events unfold in time, but God sees them from the standpoint of eternity.

Obviously, this a topic to which we will have to return in a future chapter.

The Christian Hope

According to Voltaire, we are insects living for a few seconds on atoms of mud, and cannot understand the designs of an infinite Creator. And he is quite right—if we reject the Bible, as he did. But in doing so, we are left without promises and without hope. If we have no Word from the Creator, the world of nature is a brute fact, revealing no hidden messages. Left to ourselves, we could never figure out the meaning of our existence, much less the purpose of pain. William James put it honestly when he said that we are like dogs in a library, seeing the print but unable to read the words.

> There is a vast difference between the world God originally created and the one that erupts with earthquakes, mudslides, and floods.

But when we turn to the Bible, we are offered insight; not all of our questions are answered, but at least we can see that God has not overlooked the flaws on His planet. He is neither indifferent nor unaware of what has gone wrong with nature. For openers, there is a vast difference between the world God originally created and the one that erupts with earthquakes, mudslides, and floods. Something is out of joint, and our world awaits God to make it right. We are living on a once perfect but now flawed planet. Sin changed everything.

Here is the way Paul put it in Romans:

> I consider that our present sufferings are not worth comparing with the glory that will be revealed in us. The creation waits in eager expectation for the sons of God to be revealed. For the creation was subjected to frustration, not by its own

choice, but by the will of the one who subjected it, in hope that the creation itself will be liberated from its bondage to decay and brought into the glorious freedom of the children of God. We know that the whole creation has been groaning as in the pains of childbirth right up to the present time.

ROMANS 8:18-22

Paul begins by saying that this present suffering can't compare to the future glory of those who know God. Suffering is redeemable; the future will make up for the present. The last chapter has yet to be written. Answers that elude us in this life might be answered in the next.

Paul then connects the curse of nature with man's sin. He points out that man's state of sin was his own doing, but God subjected nature to the curse even though it had no part in the decision: "For the creation was subjected to frustration, not by its own choice." Mankind, now tainted with sin, could not live in a perfect sinless environment. So Creation became an impersonal victim of Adam's personal choice to rebel.

Nature is cursed because man is cursed; natural evil—if we call it such—is therefore a reflection of moral evil, in that both are savage, ruthless, and damaging. Nature is not as bad as it could be: Rain is followed by sunshine, a tsunami is followed by calm, and eventually an earthquake is followed by stillness. Just so, we as human beings are not as evil as we could be. But we are a mixture of good and evil, and all too often evil takes the upper hand. Nature is therefore a mirror in which we see ourselves.

When we look at Hurricane Katrina we should see a picture of the evil side of human nature—powerful, heartless, and randomly cruel. In an age that is indifferent to sin, natural disasters hold up a mirror that tells us what our sin looks like to God. Sin always leaves a trail of death and destruction with ongoing painful consequences. Both the physical world and mankind await a liberation that only God can bring about.

We can engage in a fight against nature because we are armed with the knowledge that this world is not normal; it is not what it once was. So we fight disease, subdue weeds, and use fuel to warm our homes. We cooperate with nature when we can, and subdue it to our benefit. Just so, we also fight against sin in our own lives, within our nation, and within the world. We fight the curse wherever it might be found.

> God has promised to transform this present world by removing the curse of sin and bringing about an eternity of justice and righteousness.

The creation "waits in eager expectation" for its deliverance. The Greek word used in this verse fittingly describes the attitude of a man who scans the horizon searching for the first glimpse of the dawn break of glory.[10] Nature is pictured as if on tiptoes, waiting for its own release from the curse. Someday it will be "brought into the glorious freedom of the children of God." God will not allow redeemed people to live in an unredeemed environment. So when God's people are fully and finally redeemed, nature will follow suit. Better days lie ahead.

We can agree with Voltaire on one point: From our point of view, this is not the best of all possible worlds. But we also strongly affirm that God has promised to transform this present world by removing the curse of sin and bringing about an eternity of justice and righteousness. We have the possibility of such hope only if an intelligent, powerful God is behind what we see on our TV screens when a city lies in ruins.

Wind, Rain, and a Collapsed House

The Lisbon earthquake split Europe between earth and heaven.[11] On the one hand, the tragedy stimulated interest in the comforts of religion, especially the Christian faith. Church attendance increased and people were more likely to be attentive to eternity, and loyal to the church and God. But it also spurred the development of naturalism and the growth of the secular Enlightenment.

The great philosopher Immanuel Kant wrote a book about the disaster and concluded that earthquakes could be scientifically explained using physics and chemistry. He argued that there was no need to bring God into the discussion about the cause of the quake, claiming that God was necessary for what could not be explained, but was quite unnecessary once it was determined that nature was behaving according to various natural laws of physical motion.

The Lisbon quake forced a decision: The heavenly minded were motivated to become more devoted to their religious commitments; the earthly minded were more inclined to explain all of life without reference to a God who interacted with the world. In other words, people made a choice to either turn to God, or to turn away from Him in disappointment and anger. Those who turned away did so because they trusted their own opinions more than those of the Bible.

Natural disasters have a way of dividing humanity, getting to the bottom of our values and character. They have a way of revealing our secret loves and personal convictions. Jesus told a story about a natural disaster that exposed the inner lives of two neighbors.

> Therefore everyone who hears these words of mine and puts them into practice is like a wise man who built his house on the rock. The rain came down, the streams rose, and the winds blew and beat against that house; yet it did not fall, because it had its foundation on the rock. But everyone who hears these words of mine and does not put them into practice is like a foolish man who built his house on sand. The rain came down, the streams rose, and the winds blew and beat against that house, and it fell with a great crash.
>
> **MATTHEW 7:24-27**

Consider that on a beautiful sunny afternoon, these two houses looked identical. Only the powerful wind distinguished between the two. Disasters clarify our values, challenge our faith, and reveal who we really are. If we are rooted in the promises of Jesus, we can endure. If not, we will be swept away by our own human philosophies and narrow interpretations.

To those who find themselves distantly related to God—God as an idea, God as a construct, God as a last resort in difficulty—natural disasters are only a further reason to disbelieve in God and His care. But as for those who have tested God by His Word and His promises, their faith will survive the onslaught of past disasters as well as those that are yet to come.

This brief introduction to natural disasters serves two purposes: First, we must be warned to not quickly read into these events our own specific view of what God is up to. We've already learned that people will always give these disasters an interpretation compatible with their religion, their understanding of sin, and their own convictions of what they think God should do. Let's avoid these extremes.

But let us not go to the opposite extreme and speak as if the Bible is silent about these matters. I disagree with Eastern Orthodox theologian David B. Hart, who is quoted in the *Wall Street Journal* as saying that we are not warranted to "utter odious banalities about God's inscrutable counsels or blasphemous suggestions that all this mysteriously serves God's good ends."[12]

If natural disasters do not serve God's good ends, then we are either confronted with a God who is too weak to make evil serve higher ends, or too evil to do what is good and just. Yes, there is a great danger in claiming to know too much about God's purpose. But there is also a danger of being silent, of not saying what the Bible allows us to say about these horrific events. Natural disasters do have an important message that we dare not ignore.

Second, we must realize that to ask why natural disasters happen is similar to asking why people die. Six thousand people die every hour on this planet, most of them in anguish—much like those who die in an earthquake or tidal wave. Many more children die of starvation every day than the total number of people who died when Hurricane Katrina struck the Gulf Coast. The only reason natural disasters attract our attention is that they dramatically intensify the daily occurrence of death and destruction. Like death itself, natural disasters will be with us until God transforms the present order. And, as I shall explain later, the worst natural disasters still lie ahead.

In the next chapter we turn to the question of God's relationship to natural disasters. Are they acts of God? Should we protect God's reputation by saying that disasters are simply the result of fallen nature? Or should we blame the devil for these acts? And what are the implications of our answers?

QUESTIONS FOR DISCUSSION

1. Do you think God wants us to search for answers regarding God's plan and natural disasters?

2. In what ways do you think natural disasters mirror the evil side of human nature?

3. How do natural disasters "get to the bottom of our values and character," exposing our inner life?

4. What do you think of Immanuel Kant's idea that if natural disasters can be explained by natural laws, it is unnecessary to bring God into the discussion?

CHAPTER 2

IS GOD RESPONSIBLE?

I'm told that after an earthquake in California a group of ministers met for a prayer breakfast. As they discussed impassable expressways and ruined buildings, they agreed that for all practical purposes, God had nothing to do with this disaster. The earth is fallen, they concluded, so earthquakes simply happen according to certain laws of the natural order. Yet, surprisingly, when one of the ministers closed in prayer, he *thanked God* for the timing of the earthquake that came at 5:00 in the morning when there were fewer cars on the expressways than at a later time and the sidewalks were largely empty. When he finished the prayer, his colleagues chimed in with a hearty "Amen."

So, did God have anything to do with that earthquake or didn't He? Why should anyone thank God for the timing of an earthquake if He was but an "interested observer"? Why should we ever pray that we would be delivered out of such a calamity if God is not directly connected to what is happening in this fallen world?

Intuitively, people know God is in charge.

"No, God! No, God! No, God!"

Those are the words of a man who apparently thought God had *something* to do with Hurricane Katrina. He was one of many who prayed as he climbed into his attic to wait out the high waters and the storm. Many people who had not prayed in years (if ever) called out to God when that tragedy struck.

Tornadoes are quite frequent in certain areas of the United States. In 1999, hundreds of homeless families sifted through rubble after dozens of furious tornadoes ripped through Oklahoma and parts of Kansas. One huge funnel cloud skipped across the ground for four hours, killing at least forty-three people and destroying more than fifteen hundred homes and hundreds of businesses. That storm was classified F5, the most powerful tornado there is, with winds of more than two hundred fifty miles per hour.[1]

Statistics alone are quite meaningless. But think of the two-year-old child ripped from his father's hands, thrown dozens of feet into the air before being slammed against the ground. Or imagine the father who crawled into a tornado shelter only to drown when it filled with water.

The tsunami of 2004 also inflicted terrible suffering on an unsuspecting populace. But I've not read a more gripping account of the agony survivors endured than this account of an earthquake in Turkey several years ago. When we read this, we can't help but feel the anguish:

The choice is between two types of hell: the one where you lie in sodden blankets in a muddy field or forest floor in the rain, or the one where you find any shelter on the pavements of the cities and sleep among the ruins where the rats are flourishing and the dead still lie in their thousands.

The lost people of this devastated two hundred-mile industrialized corridor of northwestern Turkey have made their choice. They are going into the hills in increasing numbers. Terrified and traumatized to the point where they can barely feel any grief for those who have died, they have only one thought—to get away from these obscene places they once called home.

As each hour passes, what were once bustling towns are being emptied as more than 250,000 people accept that life there is no longer possible. So great is the damage that four major towns . . . have to be razed. Not a single house in a chain of communities stretching from Istanbul to Adapazari is safe to occupy. . . .

Yesterday it again rained without stopping. Those still remaining here covered themselves in black bin-liners and sheets, and either wandered like black and white ghosts, or tried to sleep wherever they could.[2]

Before we discuss God's role in these tragedies, we should pause and mourn for the horrendous pain people experience on this planet. Like the weeping prophet Jeremiah, we find ourselves saying, "Arise, cry out in the night, as the watches of the night begin; pour out your heart like water in the presence of the Lord. Lift up your hands to him for the lives of your children, who faint from hunger at the head of every street" (Lamentations 2:19).

We simply can't comprehend the magnitude of such disasters. We think of the tidal waves in Honduras in 1998 that killed twenty-five thousand people and left a half million homeless. The following December, mudslides in Venezuela killed an estimated fifty thousand in just a few days. On television we see the poverty, the orphans, the dirty water, and the devastated cities. After a few days the news bulletins subside, but the distraught people, bless them, live with the tragedies for the rest of their lives.

Should We Absolve God of Responsibility?

Because natural disasters in and of themselves appear to reflect very unfavorably on God, it is quite understandable that many people—I'm speaking about Christians—want to absolve Him of any and all responsibility for these horrific events. Clearly put, they want to "get Him off the hook" in order to maintain His more loving image. In the interest of protecting His reputation, many have attempted to put as much distance as possible between nature and God. Some do so by speaking of God as the caring bystander. Others present a weak God who can do little about our calamities, or a God who is bested by the devil.

Let's begin with those who have opted for a weak God, a deity who is apparently unable to prevent our planet from getting pounded by one calamity after another. Tony Campolo fears that if we say God is responsible for natural disasters, or that He does this because of a higher purpose, we will drive people away from the Christian faith. He says that since God is not the author of evil, we would do well to listen to the likes of Rabbi Harold Kushner "who contends that God is not really as powerful as we have claimed. Nowhere in the Hebrew Scriptures does it say that God is omnipotent. Kushner points out that omnipotence is a Greek philosophical concept, but it is not in his Bible. Instead, the Hebrew Bible contends that God is mighty. That means that God is a greater force in the universe than all the other forces combined."

Campolo points to the Hebrew Bible, which he believes says that God is mighty but not omnipotent. This creates a cosmic struggle between the forces of darkness and the forces of light. The good news is that God will win in the end, but for now, "When the floods swept into the Gulf Coast," Campolo writes, "God was the first one who wept."[3]

I agree with Campolo that a glib statement about suffering being part of God's plan will not immediately comfort the grieving. Such answers devoid of human compassion and understanding will drive people away from God rather than toward Him. Sometimes it is best that we be silent, not pretending that we have the right to speak on God's behalf, but to *act* benevolently on His behalf instead. Later in this book, we'll discuss in more detail how we can help victims interpret calamities. But I must say that if human suffering is not a part of God's divine plan, we need to be very fearful, since we don't know what else is going wrong in His universe that is not part of His plan.

Tony Campolo reminds me of William James, the famous American educator, who taught that evil existed because God could not overcome it—but perhaps with our help, eventually it would be overcome and light would cause the darkness to vanish. Unfortunately, James, humanist that he was, could not give us the assurance that God will win, since it appears that the conflicting powers are rather evenly matched.

Perhaps you have heard of the so-called "openness of God" controversy that has divided evangelicals. Some hold that the future is "open" to God because His knowledge is limited. They claim He does not know beforehand exactly what is going to happen at any given moment. Our decisions are particularly unknown to Him, since we are free agents, and not even He knows how we are going to choose until we have actually made our choice. Nor, they say, can He know how all the natural forces will behave until they do; He watches what happens much like we do. In this interpretation of the Bible, God would have been surprised at what happened when Hurricane Katrina struck, and would simply have wept until He decided what to do.

Just so, Tony Campolo writes of a God who is not omnipotent and who must deal with Katrina as best He can after the fact; a God who weeps, but needs time to act. How can a God like this be trusted? To be sure, Campolo assures us that God will win in the end, but how can he be sure? If God is helpless in the face of a hurricane, how confident can we be that He will subdue all the forces of nature and the devil in the end? To believe that God is finite might get Him off the hook for Katrina, but it also puts end-time victories in jeopardy. If the best He can do is weep for us, we're inclined to weep with Him, and perhaps even *for* Him.

More to the point: Doesn't the Old Testament teach that God is omnipotent? It would be strange indeed if the God who created the world were unable to subdue it. Surely even a God who was merely mighty could have prevented natural disasters of all types. And, even if the Old Testament were unclear on the question of God's power (which it is not), isn't the New Testament decisive on this point? To posit an impotent God who can only weep is hardly comforting, nor is it biblical.[4]

There is a second way that some Christians try to exempt God from involvement in natural disasters. They teach that the devil is to blame for calamities. God is not responsible for what happens. He created the world and lets it run according to certain laws, they say; nature is fallen, and Satan, who is the god of this world, wreaks havoc with the natural order.

We've already learned that nature is indeed fallen: "Cursed is the ground because of you; through painful toil you will eat of it all the days of your life. It will produce thorns and thistles for you, and you will eat the plants of the field" (Genesis 3:17-18). I once heard a story about a man who spent a great deal of his time beautifying the landscape and tending a flower garden. A friend stopped by, admired the site, and said, "My, what a wonder God created here!" To which the gardener replied, "Well, yes, but you should have seen what it looked like when God had it by Himself!" It's true: If we want beauty and symmetry on this cursed earth, we must constantly tend the garden.

Scripture clearly supports the idea that nature is fallen and that Satan might indeed be involved in natural disasters. We have an example of this in the book of Job, when God gave Satan the power to destroy Job's children. Acting under God's direction and prescribed limitations, Satan used lightning to kill the sheep and the servants, and a windstorm to kill all ten of Job's children. Here is proof, if proof is needed, that satanic powers might indeed be connected to the natural disasters that afflict our planet.

What conclusion should we draw from this? Does this mean that God is removed from nature? Does He really have a "hands-off policy" when it comes to these tragedies? Does this absolve God of responsibility? Clearly the answer is *no*.

We must think carefully at this point. We must distinguish between the *immediate* cause of these events and their *ultimate* cause. The immediate cause of the lightning and the wind that killed Job's children was the power of Satan. But follow carefully: It was God who gave Satan the power to wreak the havoc, and it was God who prescribed the limits of what Satan could or could not do. That's why Job, quite rightly, did not ascribe the death of his children to the devil but rather said, "The LORD gave and the LORD has taken away; may the name of the LORD be praised" (Job 1:21, italics added).

From a natural point of view, the immediate cause of an earthquake is a fault beneath the earth's crust; specifically, the top of the earth's crust moves in one direction while the lower plates gradually move in the opposite direction. The immediate causes of a tornado are unstable atmospheric conditions combined with warm, moist air. A hurricane forms when a large air mass is heated and fueled by the warmth of the ocean. All of these weather patterns might or might not receive their impetus from Satan, yet we can be sure that the ultimate cause of these events is God. He either rules nature directly or through secondary causes, but either way, He is in charge. After all, He is the Creator, the Sustainer, of all things. We sing with Isaac Watts,

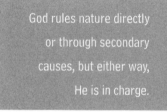

God rules nature directly or through secondary causes, but either way, He is in charge.

> *There's not a plant or flower below,*
> *But makes Thy glories known;*
> *And clouds arise, and tempests blow,*
> *By order from Thy throne.*

God has not relegated calamities to His hapless archrival the devil without maintaining strict supervision and ultimate control of nature. No earthquake comes, no tornado rages, and no tsunami washes villages away, but that God signs off on it.

First, many theologians who agree that God is in charge of nature emphasize that God does not *ordain* natural disasters but only *permits* them to happen. This might be helpful terminology, especially since in the book of Job God permitted Satan to bring about disasters to test Job. However, keep in mind that the God who permits natural disasters to happen could choose to *not* permit them to happen. In the very act of allowing them, He demonstrates that they fall within the boundaries of His providence and will. Martin Luther was right when he said that even the devil is God's devil.

Second—and this is important—God is sometimes pictured as being in control of nature, even without secondary causes. When the disciples were at wits' end, expecting to drown in a stormy sea, Christ awoke from His nap and said to the waves, "Quiet! Be still!" The effect was immediate: "Then the wind died down and it was completely calm" (Mark 4:39).

The same Christ could have spoken similar words to the tidal waves in Honduras or the rain that triggered the mudslides in Venezuela, and they would have obeyed Him. At the word of Christ, the tsunami in Southeast Asia would have ended before it began. Notice how the Scriptures ascribe tidal waves and tsunamis to God. "He who builds his lofty palace in the heavens and sets its foundation on the earth, who calls for the waters of the sea and pours them out over the face of the land—the LORD is his name" (Amos 9:6).

Third, if the heavens declare the glory of God, if it is true that the Lord reveals His attributes through the positive side of nature, doesn't it stand to reason that the calamities of nature also reveal something about His other attributes? There is no hint in the Bible that the God who created the stars and keeps them in line is somehow removed from nature. If nature is to give us a balanced picture of God, we must see His judgment, too. "The LORD does whatever pleases him, in the heavens and on the earth, in the seas and all their depths. He makes clouds rise from the ends of the earth; he sends lightning with the rain and brings out the wind from his storehouses" (Psalm 135:6-7).

We shall revisit this idea in the next chapter.

Calamities in the Bible

After the tsunami, a supposed Christian cleric was asked whether God had anything to do with the disaster. "No," he replied. "The question as to why it happened demands a *geological* answer, not a *theological* answer." Is he reading the same Bible as I am? Or has he read the Bible and simply chosen not to believe it?

Who sent the flood during the time of Noah? God said, "I am going to bring floodwaters on the earth to destroy all life under the heavens, every creature that has the breath of life in it. Everything on earth will perish" (Genesis 6:17). God determined the timing, the duration, and the intensity of the rain. And it happened according to His Word. It would have been difficult to convince Noah that God had nothing to do with the weather, so the best He could do would be to weep when the flood came.

Who sent the plagues of Egypt, the hail and darkness that could be felt? Who caused the sun to stand still so that Joshua could win a war? Who sealed the heavens during the time of Elijah and then brought rain in response to his prayer? Who sent the earthquake when the sons of Korah rebelled against Moses? This event is of special interest:

> As soon as [Moses] finished saying all this, the ground under them split apart and the earth opened its mouth and swallowed them, with their households and all Korah's men and all their possessions. They went down alive into the grave, with everything they owned; the earth closed over them, and they perished and were gone from the community.
>
> **NUMBERS 16:31-33**

Can anyone say that God is not the ultimate cause of these disasters?

The biblical writer leaves no doubt as to who caused the storm that forced the sailors to throw Jonah overboard. "Then *the LORD* sent a great wind on the sea, and such a violent storm arose that the ship threatened to break up" (Jonah 1:4, italics added). The sailors agonized about unloading their unwanted cargo, but we read, "Then they took Jonah and threw him overboard, and the raging sea grew calm" (v. 15). It appears that the Bible is not as concerned about God's reputation as some theologians are. It puts God clearly in charge of the wind, the rain, and the calamities of the earth.

What do all these stories have in common? First, we notice that God is meticulously involved. Whether an earthquake, a raging wind, or a rainstorm, the events came and left according to God's Word. Second, these were, for the most part, acts of judgment. They were the means by which God expressed His hatred for disobedience. In Old Testament times, these judgments generally separated the righteous from the wicked (this is not the case today, as we shall see in the next chapter). However, even back then sometimes the righteous were victims of these judgments too. Job's children were killed, not because they were wicked, but because God wanted to test their father.

On the other hand, we should also note that in both the Old and New Testaments God sent an earthquake to *help* His people. In the course of battle, Saul's son Jonathan killed a Philistine, and we read, "Then panic struck the whole army—those in the camp and field, and those in the outposts and raiding parties—*and the ground shook. It was a panic sent by God*" (1 Samuel 14:15, italics added).

And in the New Testament, an earthquake delivered Paul and Silas from prison. "About midnight Paul and Silas were

praying and singing hymns to God, and the other prisoners
were listening to them. Suddenly there was such a violent
earthquake that the foundations of the prison were shaken.
At once all the prison doors flew open, and everybody's
chains came loose" (Acts 16:25-26).

Earthquakes bear the signature of God.

But if there is still some doubt in your mind that ultimately
God has control of nature, let me ask: Have you ever prayed
for beautiful weather for a wedding? Have you ever prayed
for rain at a time of drought? Have you ever prayed for protection during a severe storm? Many people who claim God
has no control over the weather change their mind when a
funnel cloud comes toward them.
We can try to distance God from
these events, but the moment we
bow our heads to pray, we are ac-
knowledging that He is in charge.

> Many people who claim God has no control over the weather change their mind when a funnel cloud comes toward them.

The ministers in San Francisco
were right in thanking God that the
earthquake came early in the morn-
ing when there was little traffic on the expressways. They were
wrong, however, for saying that God was not responsible for
the tragedy. Of course He was. Both biblically and logically, it
can be no other way.

Most important, if nature is out of God's hands, then I am
also out of God's hands because I could be the victim of nature and thus die apart from His intentional will and purpose.

Jesus, however, assures His children that they are secure within the details of His providential care. "Are not five sparrows sold for two pennies? Yet not one of them is forgotten by God. Indeed, the very hairs of your head are all numbered. Don't be afraid; you are worth more than many sparrows" (Luke 12:6-7). The God who cares for the lilies of the field and the tiny sparrows is well in charge of nature.

Dare We Charge God with Evil?

But if God is the ultimate cause of all things, dare we charge Him with evil? Are not all His gifts good, perfect, and helpful? How can God be good when He permits (or does) things that seem so destructive and hurtful to human beings? Surely if we had the power to prevent an earthquake, if we could have stopped the tsunami, we would have done so. Think of the children who become orphans when a natural disaster strikes, as well as the new widows, the depleted resources, and the fresh graves. Is God to be blamed?

As previously mentioned, natural disasters are not evil in the usual sense of the term. If a tsunami were to take place in the middle of the ocean and not affect us humans, we would not think of it as an occurrence of evil. It's when humans are affected that such disasters become evil because they cause human suffering.

Yet, we must honestly face the question, should God be blamed for such destructive disasters that create unfathomable human suffering? That word *blame* implies wrongdoing,

and I don't believe such a word should ever be applied to the
Almighty. Even saying that God is responsible for natural disasters might not be best since the word *responsibility* usually
implies accountability. God, however, is accountable to no
one: "Our God is in heaven; he does whatever pleases him"
(Psalm 115:3). It is best, I believe, to say simply that God is in
charge of what happens on His planet, either directly or
through secondary causes.

Let's begin by candidly agreeing that God plays by a different set of rules. If you were standing beside a swimming
pool and watched a toddler fall in but did not pull the child
out, your negligence would be cause for prosecution. Yet God
watches children drown, or for that matter, starve, every day
and does not intervene. He sends drought to countries in Af-
rica, creating scarcity of food; He sends tidal waves, wiping
out homes and crops.

We are obligated to keep people alive as long as possible,
but if God were held to that standard, no one would ever die.
He could keep the whole population of the world alive indefinitely. What for us would be criminal is an everyday occurrence for God.

Why the difference? He is the Creator; we are the crea-
tures. Because He is the Giver of life, He also has the right to
take life. He has a long-term agenda that is much more com-
plex than keeping people alive as long as possible. Death and
destruction are a part of His plan. "'For my thoughts are not
your thoughts, neither are your ways my ways,' declares the

LORD. 'As the heavens are higher than the earth, so are my ways higher than your ways and my thoughts than your thoughts'" (Isaiah 55:8-9).

Not all of the Ten Commandments apply to God. For example, He cannot steal for He owns everything. Having neither father nor mother, He must of necessity honor only Himself. God does not often strike a person dead, but through disease, disaster, and various other calamities He does "take human life" regularly—daily, hourly.

The famous philosopher, John Stuart Mill, wrote that natural disasters prove that God cannot be both good and omnipotent, for if He were, suffering and happiness would be meticulously dispensed to the world, each getting exactly what he or she deserved. Given the randomness of natural disasters, Mill writes, "Not even on the most distorted and contracted theory of good which ever was framed by religious or philosophical fanaticism can the government of Nature be made to resemble the work of a being at once both good and omnipotent."[5]

Mill forgets, however, a second principle: that final rewards and punishments are not meted out in this life. Indeed, the Scriptures teach that the righteous often endure the most fearful calamities. God always acts from the standpoint of eternity rather than time, and all decisions are made with an infinite perspective. If you were to think of a measuring tape that goes to the farthest star, the planet Earth would only be a hairline on that tape. Thus, what we view from the standpoint of time, God sees in a vast panorama of eternity. There will be plenty of time for punishment and reward.

We believe that God has a good and all-wise purpose for the heartrending tragedies disasters bring. Speaking of the earthquake in Turkey that took thousands of lives, John Piper says, "[God] had hundreds of thousands of purposes, most of which will remain hidden to us until we are able to grasp them at the end of the age."[6] God must have a purpose for each individual, whether dead or alive. For some, His purpose is that the deadline for final judgment has arrived; for the survivors there is extended mercy in the wake of rearranged priorities and a new focus on what really matters. The woman who said that she lost everything but God during Hurricane Katrina probably spoke for hundreds of thousands of people who turned to the Almighty in their utter despair.

God does not delight in the suffering of humanity. Surely this would be inconsistent with His basic nature of caring about the world. "But you, O Lord, are a compassionate and gracious God, slow to anger, abounding in love and faithfulness" (Psalm 86:15). God does not delight in the death of the wicked but is pleased when they turn from their wicked ways (see Ezekiel 18:23).

On the other hand, God does take delight in executing His judgments. "Just as it pleased the LORD to make you prosper and increase in number, so it will please him to ruin and destroy you. You will be uprooted from the land you are entering to possess" (Deuteronomy 28:63). The reason is obvious: He delights in defending His glory and He is jealous for the honor of His people. We'll spend more time on this in the next chapter.

Finally, as finite beings we cannot judge an infinite being. God is not obligated to tell us all that He is up to. As Paul reminded an imaginary objector to God's sovereignty, the clay has no right to judge the potter (see Romans 9:21). It is not necessary for us to

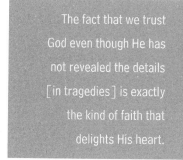

The fact that we trust God even though He has not revealed the details [in tragedies] is exactly the kind of faith that delights His heart.

know God's purposes before we bow before His authority. And the fact that we trust God even though He has not revealed the details is exactly the kind of faith that delights His heart. "And without faith it is impossible to please God" (Hebrews 11:6).

If you are adverse to what I have just written, keep in mind that God did not choose His own attributes; He simply possessed them from all of eternity. It does little good for us to object to what He chooses to do. When He said to Moses, "I AM that I AM" He in effect said *I am Who I am and not Who you would prefer Me to be.*

And yet, in chapter 4 we shall see that this sovereign God has given us reasons to trust Him. Faith will always be necessary, but our faith has strong supports. We do not believe clever fables but rather a credible account of God's will and dealings with us as found in the Bible.

Responding with Compassion

God uses nature to both bless us and challenge us, to feed us and instruct us. He intends that we strive against nature, even as we strive against the devil, so that we might become overcomers in this fallen world. Although nature is under God's supervision, we are invited to fight disease and plagues. We can and should strive for better medical care and clean water and food for the starving in third world countries. We should be willing to help those who are in distress even at great personal risk.

Martin Luther, when asked whether Christians should help the sick and dying when the plague came to Wittenburg, said that each individual would have to answer the question for himself. He believed that the epidemic was spread by evil spirits, but "Nevertheless, this is God's decree and punishment to which we must patiently submit and serve our neighbor, risking our lives in this manner as St. John teaches, 'If Christ laid down his life for us, we ought to lay down our lives for the brethren' (1 John 3:16)."[7]

As I write these words, the news media is carrying stories about avian influenza (bird flu), which could come to the United States with the potential of infecting humans. Some Christians might wonder whether they should flee or stay to help those who are sick, risking their own lives for the sake of others. Disasters such as these make Luther's comments about the Wittenberg plague very relevant. He continues:

If it be God's will that evil come upon us and destroy
us, none of our precautions will help us. Everybody
must take this to heart: first of all, if he feels bound
to remain where death rages in order to serve his neighbor, let him commend himself to God and say, "Lord,
I am in thy hands; thou hast kept me here; thy will be
done. I am thy lowly creature. Thou canst kill me or
preserve me in the pestilence in the same way as if
I were in fire, water, drought or any other danger."[8]

Yes, the plague was "God's decree," but we also must do
what we can to save the lives of the sick and minister to the
dying. We should thank God
when He gives us the opportunity
to rescue the wounded when a disaster strikes. Tragedies give us
the opportunity of serving the living and the dying all around us.
Through the tragedies of others,
we have the opportunity to be
pried from our comfortable life-
styles and enter the suffering of the world.

> Through the tragedies
> of others, we have the
> opportunity to be pried from
> our comfortable lifestyles
> and enter the suffering
> of the world.

Historically, the church has always responded to tragedies
with sacrifice and courage. During the third century,
Tertullian wrote that when pagans deserted their nearest relatives in the plague, Christians ministered to the sick. And
when the pagans left their fallen unburied in the fields of

battle, Christians risked their lives to retrieve the bodies and to relieve the suffering of the wounded.

When Hurricane Katrina hit the Gulf Coast, churches rose to the occasion to help the victims. Tens of thousands of meals were prepared, and churches helped other churches begin the painful process of relocation and reconstruction. Even the secular press had to admit that red tape did not stop the churches from sacrificially helping in time of need. What the government and the Red Cross could not do, the people of God did. This is how it should be.

Jesus was touched by the plight that the curse of sin brought to this world. We see Him weep at the tomb of Lazarus, and we hear His groans. "Jesus, once more deeply moved, came to the tomb. It was a cave with a stone laid across the entrance" (John 11:38). After the stone was removed, Jesus shouted, "Lazarus, come out!" and the dead man came to life in the presence of the startled onlookers. The very same Jesus who stayed away for a few extra days so Lazarus would die is the very same Jesus who raised him from the dead.

Just so, the very same God who created the laws of nature and allows them to "take their course" is the very same God who commands us to fight against these natural forces. The mandate that Adam and Eve were given to rule over nature before the Fall continued, but now the ground would yield thorns and thistles, and childbearing would mean struggling with pain. The desire to live would become the fight to live.

Although modern medicine and technology allow us to

stave off death as long as possible, eventually we will all be overcome by its power. Yet in the end we win, for Christ came to conquer the decay of fallen nature.

There is, perhaps, no greater mystery than the whys and wherefores of human suffering, so let us humbly confess that God's ways are past finding out.

William Cowper put the mysteries of God in perspective:

God moves in a mysterious way
His wonders to perform
He plants His footsteps in the sea,
And rides upon the storm.

Deep in unfathomable mines
Of never-failing skill
He treasures up His bright designs,
And works His sovereign will.

Ye fearful saints, fresh courage take,
The clouds ye so much dread
Are big with mercy, and shall break
In blessing on your head.

Judge not the Lord by feeble sense,
But trust Him for His grace
Behind a frowning providence
He hides a smiling face.

His purposes will ripen fast,
Unfolding every hour;
The bud may have a bitter taste,
But sweet will be the flower.

Blind unbelief is sure to err,
And scan His work in vain;
God is His own interpreter
And He will make it plain.[9]

"Grieve not because thou understandest not life's mystery," wrote a wise man. "Behind the veil is concealed many a delight."[10] The trusting believer knows this is so.

QUESTIONS FOR DISCUSSION

1. Does the idea of a God who "weeps" give you comfort? What are the negative implications of believing in such a God?

2. What's the difference between intermediate causes and ultimate causes? How do you see this played out in natural disasters?

3. Do you believe that God could use a natural disaster for good? Why or why not?

4. List several ways in which God is different from us—both in His person and His purposes for us and the world.

CHAPTER 3

ARE THERE LESSONS
TO BE LEARNED?

Created as we are in the image of God, we are inclined to probe the hidden purposes of the Almighty in allowing (hence, in fact, ordaining) human tragedy. We must be cautious, not pretending to know more than we do, but we must also refrain from the opposite mistake of saying nothing at all.

I must emphasize that when I speak about "lessons to be learned" from natural disasters, I do not mean to imply that I am giving *reasons* that God sends these devastations to the world. Ultimately, only He knows the real reasons, and He has not seen fit to reveal the details to us. Nor do I wish to imply that these lessons will comfort those who suffer in loneliness and pain. Let us candidly admit that *even if we knew all the reasons God sent a disaster, it would not lessen the pain of a mother grieving for her children.*

When disaster comes, we must spend more time praying than talking. And yet, upon reflection, we can see that God has given us a glimmer of His purposes through His Word. I think that Jesus shed some light on the question of human tragedy when He referred to a collapsed tower under which eighteen men were buried. Here was a tragedy known and talked about in the city of Jerusalem.

It is quite possible that this tower was an aqueduct built by Romans who were employing Jews in its construction. Of course, the Jewish zealots would have disapproved of Jewish workers helping with a project that would benefit their despised oppressors. We can imagine the response: "Those men deserved to die. . . . They were victims of God's judgment!" I'm sure the self-righteous pointed fingers in those days too!

Jesus, however, gave a different interpretation of the event: "Or those eighteen who died when the tower in Siloam fell on them—do you think they were more guilty than all the others living in Jerusalem? I tell you, no! But unless you repent, you too will all perish" (Luke 13:4-5).

Disasters Happen Randomly

Jesus used the incident of the collapsed tower to point out that disasters do not separate the wicked from the righteous. Those who died were not greater sinners than others in Jerusalem. It was both morally wrong and self-righteous to sit in judgment of those who were killed so unexpectedly. From God's standpoint disasters might be meticulously planned, but from our perspective they occur haphazardly, randomly. We have no right to think they divide the human race into two separate categories of righteous and wicked.

In Old Testament times, God ruled the Jewish nation directly; so He dealt with them as a group that lived within a certain geographical area. Thus, there was often (although not always) a direct cause-and-effect relationship between their obedience and the cooperation of natural forces. God said He would use nature to reward or punish the people. "When I shut up the heavens so that there is no rain, or command locusts to devour the land or send a plague among my people, if my people, who are called by my name, will humble themselves and pray and seek my face and turn from their wicked ways, then will I hear from heaven and will forgive their sin and will heal their land" (2 Chronicles 7:13-14). Grasshoppers and plagues as a punishment for disobedience; rain and good crops as a reward for obedience.

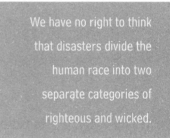

We have no right to think that disasters divide the human race into two separate categories of righteous and wicked.

Contrast this with today, when good crops are sometimes given even when a nation turns from God, as can be seen in the United States. We've often observed that just as unbelievers are blessed along with believers, so the righteous are often victims along with unbelievers. Disasters appear to come blindly and without regard to position, status, or age.

And just as natural disasters do not divide the human race into two camps based on lifestyle, they also do not prove or disprove the relative value of any religion. After the tsunami, reports began to filter in from the different religious groups, each claiming that God was on their side because they were miraculously spared.

For example, ten days after the tsunami, the *Chicago Tribune* reported that "a Sri Lankan priest's decision to leave a small coastal chapel unused on December 26 was a life-saver." For no particular reason, the priest moved the Mass from the beachside chapel to a church a mile from the coast. As a result, the service started forty-five minutes late, and when it was over, the tsunami struck. Even if the service had started on time, many of the parishioners would likely have already returned to their homes and been caught in the deadly waves. But because the Mass was performed later than scheduled, the fifteen hundred people who stayed to the end of the service survived.[1]

The priest himself did not say that this proves the truthfulness of the Catholic faith. But others believe the reason they were spared was because St. Joseph, the church in which the services were held, has a statue of the holy family, whereas the coastal church that was totally destroyed does not.

I also heard a story of protection from the Protestant evangelical wing of the church. In the town of Meulaboh, Indonesia, there are about four hundred Christians. They wanted to celebrate Christmas on December 25 but were not permitted to do so by the Muslims. They were told that if they wanted to honor the birth of Christ they needed to go outside the city. So the Christians left town to celebrate Christmas, spending the next night on a hill. In the morning, the tsunami killed eighty percent of the people of the village, but all the Christians were spared. According to Pastor Bill Hekman, some Muslims now believe that many of their fellow Muslims died because of how they treated the Christians who were spared. This is proof, he says, that God protects His own.[2]

But in another area where the tsunami hit, Poorima Jayaranten has a different interpretation. Four houses next to hers were flattened, while three rooms in her house are still standing intact. She explains her survival this way: "Most of the people who lost relatives were Muslim," adding for good measure that two Christians were also missing. She believes that Lord Buddha protected her, as she points to a picture of him that hangs on one of the remaining intact walls of her house, undisturbed by the massive destruction. Evidently, this is all she needs to confirm her faith.[3]

Muslims, however, can also claim victories because in one area along the coast every building was leveled as far as the eye can see—except a white mosque. Might this show the superiority of the Muslim faith? Some think so. As for Katrina, many Muslims praised "her," saying she had joined them in their fight against the United States.

My point is clear: We should not seek confirmation of any special religion in the disasters that pound our planet. Tragedies separate people into two camps—the dead and the living—but not the saved and the damned, not the religious and irreligious.

Yet, I also believe that natural disasters are God's mega-phone. He is speaking to us even if He is not saying what some people claim to be hearing. Surely disasters teach us lessons, and as we shall see in the next chapter, they can also be previews of events to come.

Lessons We Can Learn

We are not left without any clues as to what these tragedies should mean, even if God's ultimate purpose is mysterious. It would be a mistake if disasters came and went without us seeing in them—through simple observation and the teaching of Jesus—the instruction we should never forget.

I visited the Pompeii exhibit at the Field Museum in Chicago some time ago and was fascinated by what the victims left behind when Mount Vesuvius erupted in AD 79. Almost always, it seemed, people died trying to hoard the few treasures they had: necklaces, mirrors, and silver or gold coins. One display read, "Holding her family's wealth, the woman of the house died alongside her slaves." This woman tried to escape with her treasures, but alas, she died with those who owned nothing. Natural disasters have a leveling effect on humanity; at the moment of death, we are all reduced to the same helplessness.

Clarified Values

Disasters help us to see what is truly valuable and what is not: Tragedy separates the trivial from the weighty, the temporal from the eternal. When that tower in Siloam fell, no one mourned the loss of the bricks, but eighteen families mourned the loss of a husband, father, or brother.

In the wake of Hurricane Katrina, author Max Lucado said, "No one laments a lost plasma television or submerged SUV. No one runs through the streets yelling, 'My cordless drill is missing' or 'My golf clubs have washed away.' If they mourn, it is for people lost. If they rejoice, it is for people found."[4] He goes on to say that raging hurricanes and broken levees have a way of prying our fingers off the things we love. One day you have everything; the next day you have nothing.

> Disasters help us to see what is truly valuable and what is not. Tragedy separates the trivial from the weighty, the temporal from the eternal.

We are reminded of the words of Jesus: "Watch out! Be on your guard against all kinds of greed; a man's life does not consist in the abundance of his possessions" (Luke 12:15). As a pastor, I've seen how the suffering of a child or the death of a loved one suddenly gives people a whole new pair of glasses through which to view the world. True loss exposes our tendency to give first-rate attention to second-rate priorities as we awake to the realization that someday the world and everything in it will be burned up and all that will remain are angels, demons, human beings, and God.

The French philosopher Blaise Pascal was correct when he said, "Man's sensitivity to trivia, and his insensitivity to matters of major importance, reveal he has a strange disorder."[5] Only tragedy jerks us into reality and makes us realize that people matter and things don't. Tragedy divides time and eternity, this world from the next. And to further clarify our values Jesus also said, "What good will it be for a man if he gains the whole world, yet forfeits his soul?" (Matthew 16:26).

I agree with John Piper, who said that natural disasters give Christians the opportunity to prove that no earthly treasure can compare with the value of knowing Christ. It's a reminder of Paul's words: "But whatever was to my profit I now consider loss for the sake of Christ. What is more, I consider everything a loss compared to the surpassing greatness of knowing Christ Jesus my Lord, for whose sake I have lost all things. I consider them rubbish, that I may gain Christ and be found in him, not having a righteousness of my own that comes from the law, but that which is through faith in Christ" (Philippians 3:7-9). Those who know Jesus have a treasure that suffering and death can never take from them.

Mankind's Dual Nature

I've always been fascinated by human nature. I marvel at both human goodness and human evil, and how the two can sometimes exist side by side when tragedy strikes. In New Orleans, we saw many stories of heroic and sacrificial rescues, many people risking their own lives for the sake of others.

Yet, at the same time, we also saw raw human nature in all of its horridness. I'm not talking about looters who grabbed what they could for their families. I'm speaking about the rumors of rape, beatings, and murders that took place in the Superdome. I'm talking about fires being deliberately set and rescue helicopters being repeatedly fired upon. Those who returned to clean up after the disaster were surprised by the amount of pornography that was exposed when the waters flooded the streets. We should take time to ask ourselves: If we had to suddenly flee our homes, what would be left behind for others to see?

Volunteers also arrived in force after the tsunami, many making great personal sacrifices to help the victims. But at the same time, we also heard about the horrid sex trade in countries such as Thailand and Sri Lanka. After the tsunami, reports filtered through about young children being kidnapped and exploited for sexual perverts who surfaced to take advantage of these precious little ones. As if being orphaned was not enough, those children became prey for the most despicable acts of human cruelty imaginable.

As we've already seen, the world of physical nature is a reflection of the moral world of human beings. Just as the tsunami let loose a torrent of water that engulfed the land, and just as the breached levees in New Orleans released a flood of water over much of the city, so the evil of the human heart was also set free to do its damage in the midst of the disaster. If it weren't for the restraints that keep human nature in check, this world would be overwhelmed by an unstoppable tidal wave of evil.

However—and this is important—we must realize that there is a mixture of evil and goodness in all of us. It was Nobel Prize winner Aleksandr Solzhenitsyn who said that we cannot divide the human race into two camps, the good and the evil. If we could divide the race that way, he said, then we could put all the good people on one part of the planet and all the bad people on another part. Then the righteous could live in a "sin-free zone." That's not possible, of course. Solzhenitsyn correctly pointed out that the line between good and evil does not run through the human race, but through every human heart!

> The line between good and evil does not run through the human race, but through every human heart.

We all need redemption. Left to ourselves, we are filled with suspicion, greed, and fear. We will take advantage of others to enrich ourselves; we will become obsessed with self-interest, caring little for the welfare of our neighbors. Tragedy brings the good, the bad, and the ugly to the surface, and human nature is exposed for all to see. Pascal was right when he said, "There is nothing that we can see on earth which does not either show the wretchedness of man or the mercy of God."[6]

The Uncertainty of Life

Natural disasters confirm the words of James: "Why, you do not even know what will happen tomorrow. What is your life? You are a mist that appears for a little while and then vanishes" (James 4:14). People who lose their lives in a natural disaster probably do not wake that morning telling themselves, *This could be my last day on earth*. Unfortunately, few of us believe that what happened to them could happen to us. But the tower of Siloam, like a natural disaster, also fell unexpectedly, without prior warning.

When you read the obituaries of those who have died in sudden calamities, do you visualize your own name there? We all know someone who has been unexpectedly killed in an accident, perhaps in a car wreck, an accident at work, or an unexpected heart attack. When we grieve with the families, we should remind ourselves that we, too, could die at any moment. Natural disasters serve as a similar reminder that death might be just around the next corner.

I read about one couple who left California for fear of earthquakes and died in a tornado in Missouri! Life is simply a loan from God. He gives it and He takes it. And He can take it whenever and however He chooses. This sounds heartless, but C. S. Lewis was right when he pointed out that war does not really increase death; even without war, the victims would still have to die eventually. Cruel as it sounds, death is determined for all of us, whether by cancer, an accident, or a natural disaster. The Bible teaches that death is a scheduled, divine appointment. Tragedies simply rid us of the overconfidence we have that we are in control of our destinies.

Most disheartening to me were the stories of those who

died needlessly in New Orleans because they would not heed the warnings to flee. Edgar Hollingsworth refused to leave his home when Katrina was approaching. His wife, Lillian, kissed him good-bye, and although she and his grandchildren begged him to leave, he refused. "Don't worry about me," he said. "When I was in the Army I went a whole month without eating." He believed the storm would not hit his neighborhood but go around, the same way all the previous ones had.

Edgar's relatives thought of forcing him into a car, but they did not want to make him angry. "All of a sudden he got real

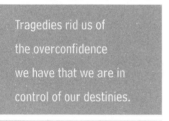

Tragedies rid us of the overconfidence we have that we are in control of our destinies.

stubborn," Lillian said. The next day the storm came and the waters rose. They tried to make contact with Edgar, but the phone lines were down and they knew they had to leave the city. Lillian prayed that someone would rescue her husband, and on some days, she felt confident that he would be fine.

Meanwhile, rescue teams had put an X and a zero on the house in which Edgar was living, indicating that they had checked the house and were confident no one was inside. But when another rescue team went to search for abandoned animals, they discovered Edgar, unclothed and almost skeletal on an upended couch. They were shocked when Edgar, whom they thought was dead, suddenly gasped for air. Emergency crews hurried to his house and immediately began life-saving measures.

The next day, Lillian stared in shock at the picture of her husband on the front page of a Baton Rouge newspaper. She found out where he had been taken and rushed to his side; but despite heroic efforts, Edgar died twenty minutes after she arrived. In retrospect, Lillian wishes that the city of New Orleans had mandated that all people be forcibly removed from their homes.[7]

Why did people stay in New Orleans, in spite of the warnings? Some said they were confident that they could climb up the stairs in their house if they had to. They did not realize that water would come up to the second floor, then the attic, and finally the rooftop.

Disasters, in the words of David Miller, remind us that "human existence on Earth was not intended to be permanent. Rather, the Creator intended life on Earth to serve as a temporary interval of time . . . in which people are given the opportunity to attend to their spiritual condition as it relates to God's will for living. Natural disasters provide people with conclusive evidence that life on Earth is brief and uncertain."[8]

The Danger of Self-Delusion

Unexpected tragedy ends the illusion that our lives are predictable and our futures certain. Many of us meander through our days believing that the good life consists of money, pleasure, and leisure, and that the not-so-good life is one of poverty, struggle, and servitude. But Jesus told a story that proved how such superficial evaluations can be deceptive. According to the story, a rich man who enjoyed life found himself in torment after he died, whereas a beggar who suffered in this life found himself in bliss (see Luke 16:19-31). This sudden reversal of fortune reminds us that our judgments of today might have to be severely revised tomorrow!

In one of his most popular books, C. S. Lewis imagines a lead demon, Screwtape, writing letters to Wormwood, a demonic underling, in order to give him advice on how to deceive humans. It would seem that war might be a great boon to the devil's strategy, but Screwtape says that Wormwood should not expect too much from the war; they can hope for a good deal of cruelty, but if the demons are not careful they might "see thousands turning . . . to the Enemy [God], while tens of thousands who do not go so far as that will nevertheless have their attention diverted from themselves to values and causes which they believe to be higher than the self."[9] In wartime, he points out, men prepare for death in ways they might not when things are going smoothly.

Then the demon continues.

> How much better for us if *all* humans died in costly
> nursing homes amid doctors who lie, nurses who lie,
> friends who lie, as we have trained them, promising life
> to the dying, encouraging the belief that sickness excuses
> every indulgence, and even, if our workers know their
> job, withholding all suggestion of a priest lest it should
> betray to the sick man his true condition![10]

Lewis believes—and I concur—that "contented worldliness" is one of the devil's best weapons during times of peace. But when disasters come, this weapon is rendered worthless. He writes, "In wartime not even a human can believe that he is going to live forever."

This is one reason we will never know all of God's purposes in natural disasters. We simply do not know the thousands or perhaps millions of spiritually "content" people who are forced to take God seriously in a time of crisis. Many survivors choose to harden their hearts against God; but others turn to Him in repentance and faith. And even to those of us who watch these calamities at a safe distance, God is saying, "Prepare for your own death. . . . it may be soon!"

While writing this chapter, I spoke with John Gerhardt, a pastor with Urban Impact Ministries in New Orleans, about the spiritual effects of Hurricane Katrina. Long after the disaster, Pastor Gerhardt continued to coordinate rebuilding efforts among the most needy in New Orleans. He says that Katrina opened people's hearts to their present needs, but also made them look beyond today to tomorrow, and beyond tomorrow to eternity. The high winds and water, he says, not only broke levees, but also broke the walls between churches—racially, economically, and geographically. Today, many are praying together and strategizing together to help rebuild the city.

The church, said Pastor Gerhardt, can do what the Red Cross and FEMA (Federal Emergency Management Agency) cannot. Believers can enter into the grief of others, pray with those left behind, and befriend the hopeless. He tells his congregation every Sunday that they not only want God to "show up," but also to "show off"—that is, they want to see His glorious work in the midst of suffering and despair. All along the Gulf Coast, people are coming to trust Christ as Savior, and others are being healed of their trauma and pessimism. Pastor Gerhardt would say that God shows up when disaster strikes.

But now we must turn our attention to a more difficult topic: Are natural disasters specific judgments of God? How should we interpret them from a divine perspective? In wrath, does God remember mercy?

Keep reading.

QUESTIONS FOR DISCUSSION

1. God dealt with His people differently in the Old Testament than He does today. Why do you think this is so?

2. What specific lessons has God taught you during the "storms" in your own life?

3. Why do you think that God sometimes chooses to treat the righteous and the unrighteous the same in this life?

4. What changes would you make in your own life if you knew you were going to die in a natural disaster within a month?

CHAPTER 4

ARE DISASTERS
THE JUDGMENT OF GOD?

Mayor Ray Nagin made headlines in 2006 when he suggested that Hurricane Katrina's pounding of New Orleans was a sign that "God is mad at America" and at black communities for tearing themselves apart with violence and political infighting. "Surely God is mad at America. He sent us hurricane after hurricane and it has destroyed and put stress on this country."

Nagin, who is black, also made further comments on Martin Luther King Day: "Surely [God] doesn't approve of us being in Iraq under false pretenses. But surely he is upset at black America also. We're not taking care of ourselves."[1] The mayor raised further eyebrows when he said that when New Orleans is rebuilt, it should be a city whose majority is black.

Setting aside his racial comments, was Ray Nagin right or wrong about hurricanes being God's judgment on America? Or, perhaps more to the point, was he partly right *and* partly wrong?

Let's return to the words of Jesus when He spoke about the collapsed tower of Siloam, "But unless you repent, you too will likewise perish" (Luke 13:3, NASB). Natural disasters are warnings of a time yet to come. Obviously, the unrepentant will not necessarily die in a similar calamity. But they *will* be carried away in sudden judgment without warning—a judgment more terrifying than a natural disaster could ever be.

Follow this thought carefully: The fact that natural disasters happen randomly without regard to race, age, religion, or lifestyle, does not mean that they cannot be present judgments and a preview of coming punishment for sin. We've all had to sit through previews in a theater while waiting for the real movie to begin. Natural disasters are a preview, a "heads up" warning that more severe judgment is just up ahead.

I disagree with Dennis Behrendt who wrote in *The New American* that natural disasters cannot be judgments because they happen indiscriminately. He writes, "There are plenty of people who have turned away from God and lead lives of sin and depravity, harming others and violating their rights. Why not just punish the murderers, the rapists, and the thieves? Surely God can differentiate between those who try to live godly lives and those who spurn both God and man alike."[2]

Of course, if God wished, He could send natural disasters only to the wicked. And we know that the upheavals of nature come to specific geographical areas regardless of the relative godliness or ungodliness of the people. But this does not mean that they cannot be judgments. The righteous can and do experience temporal punishments in this life along with the unrighteous. *Natural disasters are judgments, for the obvious reason that all death and destruction is a judgment of God.*

Even though Christ died for our sins, we as Christians will still die because of sin; and death is a judgment for sin. "For the wages of sin is death, but the gift

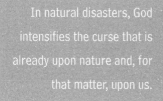

In natural disasters, God intensifies the curse that is already upon nature and, for that matter, upon us.

of God is eternal life in Christ Jesus our Lord" (Romans 6:23). Jesus removed the sting of death, but it will come to us nonetheless. Think of it this way: The whole earth is under a curse, and we as believers are a part of that corruption. Clearly, even those who are godly also become victims of tragedy and judgment in this fallen world. The curse is not fully lifted until we are fully redeemed.

In natural disasters, God intensifies the curse that is already upon nature and, for that matter, upon us. When we look at it this way, we realize that natural disasters happen every day as thousands of people die from disease, accidents, and tragedies of various kinds. Natural disasters only catch our attention when they are of great magnitude with many simultaneous deaths and unbelievable devastation to property. These disasters are really only a dramatic acceleration of what is happening all the time.

Is God Mad at America?

So, is God mad at America? Often we hear statements such as, "If we don't repent, God is going to judge America!" We forget that America is already under judgment—continuous, *present* judgment. In Deuteronomy, God warned the Jews that if they did not repent, they would experience a series of judgments, culminating in the destruction of their families. "Your sons and daughters will be given to another nation, and you will wear out your eyes watching for them day after day, powerless to lift a hand" (Deuteronomy 28:32). Indeed, children and their parents will be starving, and there will be no way to save them (see vv. 54-57).

The destruction of the family is one of God's judgments against our nation, a nation that has turned away from God. The spread of immorality, pornography, and even same-sex marriage—all of this is proof that God's hand is being removed from us as we plunge headlong into personal and national rebellion. As a result, our children are suffering from predators, from sexual abuse within their own families, and from self-absorbed, uncaring parents. All sin has immediate consequences, but when it accumulates, there are future judgments of various kinds. Natural disasters are just one more way that God reveals Himself and begs us to turn from our wicked ways and prepare for a better world.

So we are correct in saying natural disasters are judgments, but mistaken when we go beyond this and say that they target only one religion, one race, or even one particular kind of sinner. Yes, it may be true that the countries hit by the tsunami, such as Thailand and Sri Lanka, were judged because of their exploitation of children. But we must also ask, why was Bangkok spared, when it is the hub of the sex trade industry? Was New Orleans a more sinful city than Las Vegas? Only God knows for sure if the tsunami and Katrina were targeted judgments for specific sins.

As we've already seen, in this life, judgments appear to us as haphazard. Sometimes, contrary to what we would expect, the wicked are spared the catastrophes that slay the righteous. However, God has different purposes in such disasters. His purpose is for those who die to be brought into His presence where each will be judged individually, fairly, and eternally. Some will be invited into His presence and others will be banished. "Then they will go away to eternal punishment, but the righteous to eternal life" (Matthew 25:46).

> Natural disasters are just one more way that God reveals Himself and begs us to turn from our wicked ways and prepare for a better world.

His purposes for the survivors are to warn of the uncertainty of life and the urgency to prepare for death. Volunteers are given the opportunity to show their love and care for those who suffer. For some, calamities are punishment; for others, purification brought about through repentance and renewed devotion to God. What to us appears random, no doubt has specific purposes known only to the Almighty.

So we return to the question: Is God mad at America? His justifiable anger is directed at all who refuse to acknowledge His Word: "The wrath of God is being revealed from heaven against all the godlessness and wickedness of men who suppress the truth by their wickedness" (Romans 1:18). But on the other hand, He is gracious to those who respond to His mercy as found in Jesus Christ. "Since we have now been justified by his blood, how much more shall we be saved from God's wrath through him!" (Romans 5:9).

> The starry heavens reflect the glory of God; calm winds and sunshine remind us of the mercy of God; and the upheavals of nature demonstrate the judgment of God.

There are national judgments, but eventually God's focus comes down to the individual: Those who come under the protection of Christ's grace are especially loved and accepted, and those who spurn His mercy are targeted for judgment, either now or later. The good news, of course, is that all who are reading this book have a wonderful opportunity to take advantage of God's undeserved grace. "For it is by grace you have been saved, through faith—and this not from yourselves, it is the gift of God—not by works, so that no one can boast" (Ephesians 2:8-9).

When God sees America, He sees those who are under His wrath as well as those who are objects of His special grace. Yes, there comes a time when an entire nation seems to turn from God and the nation is judged. But there also is a remnant of true believers whose lives please our Father in heaven. Little wonder that we shall have to wait for eternity to bring all such matters to light.

Disasters and the End Times

Nature reflects God's gracious attributes, but also His attributes of anger and justice. In the book of Job, a discerning young theologian, Elihu, says of God, "He says to the snow, 'Fall on the earth,' and to the rain shower, 'Be a mighty downpour.' . . . The breath of God produces ice, and the broad waters become frozen. He loads the clouds with moisture; he scatters his lightning through them. At his direction they swirl around over the face of the whole earth to do whatever he commands them. He brings the clouds to punish men, or to water his earth and show his love" (Job 37:6, 10-13).

He brings clouds to punish men, or to water his earth and show his love. We like to think that God is only in control of the positive side of nature: the sunshine, the irresistible lure of calm waters, and the starry heavens. But, as we have learned, God is in charge of the totality of nature. If the goodness of God is seen in the blessings of nature, His judgments are seen in the "cursing" of nature. Either way, nature instructs us, helping us understand God better.

The starry heavens reflect the glory of God; calm winds and sunshine remind us of the mercy of God; and the upheavals of nature demonstrate the judgment of God. If the sunshine anticipates the beauty of heaven, the hurricane anticipates the suffering of hell. "Consider therefore the kindness and sternness of God: sternness to those who fell, but kindness to you, provided that you continue in his kindness" (Romans 11:22). We should not be surprised that nature is both kind and stern.

Jesus confirmed that end-time calamities were a sign of the end of the age. "There will be famines and earthquakes in various places. All these are the beginning of birth pains" (Matthew 24:7-8). Interestingly, the number of earthquakes on the earth has increased over the centuries, and their number is increasing every year. Only the powerful ones make headlines.

Depending on how you classify them, at least three—and maybe even four—natural disasters will accompany the return of Jesus to earth:

> For as lightning that comes from the east is visible even in the west, so will be the coming of the Son of Man. Wherever there is a carcass, there the vultures will gather. Immediately after the distress of those days "the sun will be darkened, and the moon will not give its light; the stars will fall from the sky, and the heavenly bodies will be shaken." At that time the sign of the Son of Man will appear in the sky, and all the nations of the earth will mourn.   **MATTHEW 24:27-30**

Let us not be too hasty in thinking that we know when and how the end will come. In 2005, a *New York Times* article titled "Doomsday: The Latest Word If Not the Last," gave some examples of how quickly Christians rush to conclusions about the end of the world.[3] We heard it when Israeli troops captured the Old City of Jerusalem in 1967, and later when Yitzhak Rabin worked out a peace accord with Yasser Arafat. And now we again hear that the end of the world is near because of the growing number of natural disasters. I have in my library a book, *The Last Days Are Here Again*. As you are no doubt aware, life on this planet has not yet ceased to exist, even though so many have predicted its demise.

Yet it is important to realize that convulsions of nature will eventually be a part of God's sovereign judgment. Consider this future "natural disaster," which appears to be the real movie that follows the preview:

> I watched as he opened the sixth seal. There was a great earthquake. The sun turned black like sackcloth made of goat hair, the whole moon turned blood red, and the stars in the sky fell to earth, as late figs drop from a fig tree when shaken by a strong wind. The sky receded like a scroll, rolling up, and every mountain and island was removed from its place. Then the kings of the earth, the princes, the generals, the rich, the mighty, and every slave and every free man hid in caves and among the rocks of the mountains. They called to the mountains and the rocks, "Fall on us and hide us from the face of him who sits on the throne and from the wrath of the Lamb! For the great day of their wrath has come, and who can stand?" **REVELATION 6:12-17**

I agree with the reader who wrote this in a letter to *World Magazine.* "We owe a great debt to those affected by Hurricane Katrina. They received just a small taste of the wrath of God as a warning to us all that unless we repent, we will all likewise perish."[4]

The God of liberal theology, the God who seeks the happiness of His creation to the best of His ability, the God who would never judge us for our sins or commit sinners to hell—such a God does not exist in the Bible. This domesticated God is contradicted by the natural disasters in the world. He does not delight in human suffering, but He does delight in the triumph of truth and justice and the completion of His hidden purposes.

The Escape Route

The good news is this: We escape coming judgment by repentance. "Unless you repent you will perish . . ." Enough has been said in this book about the danger of trying to read the details of God's purposes. So if we keep in mind that many Christians also die in these calamities, we can still profit from the words of Byron Paulus, who points out that God's message to America is to repent. He writes,

> The symbolism represented by the various locations of recent calamities is too obvious to ignore. First, terrorists attacked the national icons of our *materialistic culture.* Last year the hurricanes along the coasts

of Florida scarred a major center of *national leisure*. And now, Katrina targeted an area generally known for *sexual perversion*, as well as gambling, welfare and crime. Rita even took a shot at our *source of dependency* . . . oil. Is it a coincidence that the name Katrina means "purity"? Is God trying to get our attention?[5]

Is God Trying to Get Our Attention?

Interestingly, a few days after Hurricane Katrina, Louisiana governor Kathleen Blanco called for a statewide day of prayer: "As we face the devastation wrought by Katrina, as we search for those in need, as we comfort those in pain and as we begin the long task of rebuilding, we turn to God for strength, hope, and comfort." And New Orleans city council president Oliver Thomas, after seeing the horrific destruction firsthand and hearing comparisons of New Orleans to Sodom and Gomorrah, commented that "Maybe God's going to cleanse us."[6]

There is little doubt that New Orleans has been known as a sin city with few rivals. The New Orleans "southern decadence" festival scheduled for that weekend was

> God does not delight in human suffering, but He does delight in the triumph of truth and justice and the completion of His hidden purposes.

described by a French tourism site as "sort of like a gayer version of Mardi Gras," which is "most famous (or infamous) for the displays of naked flesh which characterize the event with public displays of sexuality." In addition to having one of the highest murder rates in the country, and the most corrupt police force, the city is also known for its widespread occult practices, particularly voodoo. As Michael Brown wrote, "When you invoke dark spirits, you get a storm."[7]

I find it interesting that although Mayor Nagin cited racial division and the war in Iraq as reasons for God's anger against America, he did not mention Mardi Gras or the widespread occultism that permeates the city. In fact, the debauchery that goes along with Mardi Gras has already returned to New Orleans as a symbol of a restored city. The mayor was right when he said that Katrina was the judgment of God, but in my opinion he was somewhat amiss in deciphering God's reasons for it. We must be careful about saying God only gets angry at the same things we get angry about.

"Perhaps God Is Cleansing Us!"

God might not have targeted New Orleans because it is more sinful than Las Vegas but there is no doubt He chose New Orleans as an object lesson for America and all of the world. Council president Oliver Thomas was right. God does want to cleanse all of America without a doubt. He is asking us to turn from all of our sins—whether immorality, greed, selfishness, or most important, the neglect of the gospel His Son came to bring us. He wants us to turn from our self-indulgence to faith in Him, the source of forgiveness and hope.

Reverend Bill Shanks of New Orleans said that after Katrina, "New Orleans is now abortion free. New Orleans is Mardi Gras free. New Orleans now is free of southern decadence and the sodomites, the witchcraft workers, false religion—free of all those things."[8] He may be right, but of course, we know that when the residents return, they will bring their sins back with them. Resolutions to change will likely give way to familiar sins.

Yes, it would be wonderful if the citizens of a restored New Orleans were to repent. But we know that as believers, we must lead the way. Peter wrote, "For it is time for judgment to begin with the family of God; and if it begins with us, what will the outcome be for those who do not obey the gospel of God? And, 'If it is hard for the righteous to be saved, what will become of the ungodly and the sinner?'" (1 Peter 4:17-18). God is shouting, but we are not listening.

Mercy is included in every act of temporal judgment. We should take a page from our brothers and sisters in Scotland who, following a 1741 hurricane, organized prayer societies. What began in one church spread to other churches, and soon the churches were filled with people praying and asking God to help them in their time of need. "People were pleading with God to multiply the work begun among them."[9]

What will it take for us to do the same?

Saved or Lost?

Natural disasters divide the human race between the dead and the living. The dead have no opportunity to repent, no second chance at life and redemption. For the living, the opportunity of repentance is still at hand. "Just as man is destined to die once, and after that to face judgment, so Christ was sacrificed once to take away the sins of many people; and he will appear a second time, not to bear sin, but to bring salvation to those who are waiting for him" (Hebrews 9:27-28).

When the *Titanic* went under, 1,516 people knowingly went to a watery grave. Even if we attribute the sinking of that ship to a series of human errors, God most assuredly could have kept it from sinking without any violation of the human will. This is another reminder that the God who permits such unthinkable tragedies is One to be feared.

After the news of the *Titanic*'s tragedy reached the world, the challenge was how to inform the relatives whether their loved ones were among the dead or the living. At the White Star Line's office in Liverpool, England, a huge board was set up; on one side was a cardboard sign: **Known To Be Saved**, and on the other, a cardboard sign with the words, **Known To Be Lost**. Hundreds of people gathered to intently watch the updates. When a messenger brought new information, those waiting held their breath, wondering to which side he would go and whose name would be added to the list.

Although the travelers on the *Titanic* were either first-, second-, or third-class passengers, after the ship went down there were only two categories: the saved and the drowned. Just so, we can divide people into many different classes based on geography, race, education, and wealth. But on the final

Day of Judgment, there will be only two classes: the saved and the lost. There is only heaven and hell.

Perhaps in heaven a mother will be looking for her son, wondering if he will arrive safely behind the pearly gates. Wives will wait for husbands, and parents for children. Today is a day of grace, a day of waiting for the living to repent.

God shouts from heaven, "Unless you repent, you will likewise perish."

QUESTIONS FOR DISCUSSION

1. Discuss the statement "Natural disasters are judgments of God." As best you can, clear up a common misunderstanding of this phrase.

2. How would you answer Ray Nagin's question: "Is God mad at America?"

3. What is the role of a Christian in the wake of natural disaster?

4. In what ways do you see natural disasters as a preview of the future?

5. What would America look like if we, as a nation, would repent of our sins?

CHAPTER 5

CAN WE STILL TRUST GOD?

Wars, poverty, natural disasters, and horrendous injustices exist on this planet. Can we trust a sovereign God who could, at any moment, put an end to such suffering? A God who could have prevented the catastrophes that have pounded the world throughout the centuries? A God who could have had Hitler die as an infant in his mother's arms?

An intellectual answer—even a true one—never satisfies the human heart. Grief is never removed when one is reminded of God's eternal and transcendent purposes. And yet we are encouraged to seek for answers, for as Ecclesiastes tells us, God has put "eternity in our hearts."

Atheism's Dead End

At the outset, one point must be clarified: Atheists (or naturalists) have no right to ask us where God is when tragedy strikes. I've often heard the argument that if a God Who is omnipotent, omniscient, and loving existed, He would do away with evil and suffering. Since horrendous suffering exists, the atheist says, God must either be weak, unknowing, or sadistic. Since such a God does not commend our respect, atheism seems to be a more attractive alternative. Atheists therefore look about, see the misery millions endure, and ask sarcastically, "Where was God when the tsunami happened?" And they defy anyone to give an answer.

The question, coming from an atheist, is illegitimate and irrational. To ask the question is to assume the existence of God. If there were not a creator God—if we are but a complicated combination of atoms that sprang into existence randomly—then the very idea of good and evil or better and best could not exist. After all, atheists believe that atoms have arranged themselves blindly according to haphazard patterns and whatever is, just *is*.

> If the atheist asks, where was God in this disaster, he is assuming a moral framework that can only exist if God exists.

So if the atheist/naturalist asks, where was God in this disaster, he is assuming a moral framework that can only exist if God exists. Based on atheistic premises, there can be no spiritual substance such as soul or mind, only patterns of physical particles. Naturalists are in the unhappy position of having to maintain that matter can think, that matter can ask questions about which arrangement of matter is good and which is bad. Clearly, notions about good or evil cannot arise from atoms that existed in primordial slime.

Carefully considered, atheism is both contrary to rationality and defies the deepest longings of the human soul. C. S. Lewis makes the same point when he argues that only God can account for the moral law that exists in all of us. During his days as an atheist, Lewis argued against God because the universe appeared so cruel and unjust. Then he realized that his idea of justice presupposed a standard that was beyond himself.

> Of course I could have given up my idea of justice by saying it was nothing but a private idea of my own. But if I did that, then my argument against God collapsed too—for the argument depended on saying that the world was really unjust, not simply that it did not happen to please my fantasies. Thus in the very act of trying to prove that God did not exist— in other words, that the whole of reality was senseless— I found I was forced to assume that one part of real- ity—namely my idea of justice—was full of sense.[1]

Lewis goes on to argue that the moral law is a better reflec- tion of God than the universe itself. He points out that the intuitive knowledge that we have of good and evil tells us more about God than nature does: "You find out more about God from the Moral Law than from the universe in general just as you find out more about man by listening to his con- versation than by looking at a house he has built."[2]

In an atheistic world, evil can never serve a higher purpose, and suffering can never be redeemed, for it can never lead to noble ends. Suicide would be attractive, for there would be no point in staying around to make this world a better place. Furthermore, in an atheistic world, the injustices of the world would just continue their senseless journey to nowhere.

A Jewish friend of mine, who is also an atheist, admitted that he felt some disquiet of spirit knowing that Hitler would never be judged for what he did. He has no hope that there will be a final judgment to set the record straight. He ruefully admitted that without eternity, the events of time can never be redeemed or made right.

Atheism satisfies neither the mind nor the heart. And yet atheists do ask questions about good and evil, for one reason: They also are created in the image of God and have a soul that can think. Ravi Zacharias says that a relativist may say that God has died, "but the question from his soul at a time like this reveals that he cannot kill Him completely."[3]

"O Katrina have mercy on us!" a sign read in New Orleans before the hurricane hit. If we do not turn to the living God in a crisis, we will turn to the impersonal god of nature or we will manufacture some other deity in our own minds. Atheism simply cannot abide for long in the thoughtful human heart.

An Intellectual Answer

So we return to this question: If God is all-powerful and has all knowledge, is He also *good*? Does He deserve our trust? If we answer yes—and I hope we do—we must affirm that there is a morally sufficient reason for God to allow (or ordain) the disasters we see, whether caused by nature or human beings. If there were no higher purpose in these evils, the Almighty would be operating blindly, making the best of tragic events but unsure of His overall plan.

The Bible stands in stark opposition to Rowan Williams, the archbishop of Canterbury who wrote dismissively about the "vacuous words pouring out about the nature of God's power or control, or about the consolations of belief in an afterlife or whatever. . . . Every single random, accidental death . . . should upset a faith bound up with comfort and ready answers."[4]

Contrary to the archbishop, I believe we *should* speak about God's power and control, and we console ourselves with the certainty of an afterlife. Although I agree that we should be wary about "ready answers," I also believe that we should not have our faith upset by every random, accidental death. I must emphasize the point we discussed earlier: If natural disasters are out of God's control, then my life and my future are out of God's control. The weak God of modern liberalism is hardly able to speak comfort to those who seek it.

At this point, we must return to the question raised in the first chapter: Is this the best of all possible worlds? Remember, the philosopher Leibniz said that a good God would choose the best of all possible worlds, so why did He chose *this* world, with its suffering and despair? Can this really be the best of all possible worlds?

Viewed through a narrow lens, this most assuredly is *not* the best of all possible worlds. But if we saw everything from God's viewpoint—if we could see the ultimate end of God's purposes and His own glory—we would have to agree that His plan is right and good. This is not the best of all possible worlds, but from the standpoint of eternity, the best of all Architects chose the best of all possible blueprints. This does not mean that God is pleased with evil, but it does mean that He is pleased with how He will use it toward wise and good ends.

What would you do if you had God's power for twenty-four hours? Of course we all answer that we would rid the world of poverty, wars, and disasters of every type. We would put an end to all forms of evil and create a paradise for everyone. *If only!*

On the other hand, if we were also given God's wisdom, I'm convinced that we would leave things as they are! For our all-wise and all-powerful heavenly Father has a hidden agenda that makes sense out of it all. There is meaning in the madness.[5]

However—and this is important—if we wonder what God's ultimate, hidden purpose is in natural disasters, we can only say that He is relentless in the pursuit of His own glory (see Jeremiah 13:11; 2 Thessalonians 1:9-10). We've already acknowledged that God does allow us some insight into the divine mind, but let us humbly confess that we see only glimpses of the eternal purpose.

After years of studying the problem of reconciling the suffering of this world with God's mercy, I have concluded that there is no solution that will completely satisfy our minds, much less the mind of a skeptic. God's ways are "past finding out." He has simply not chosen to reveal all the pieces of the puzzle. *God is more inscrutable than we care to admit.*

After all the theological essays have been written and all of the debaters have become silent, we still do not understand. We can only stand in awe of this great mystery. John Stackhouse has written,

> The God of predestination, the God of worldwide
> providence, the God who created all and sustains
> all and thus ultimately is responsible for all—this God
> has revealed to us only glimpses of the divine cosmic
> plan. God has not let us see in any comprehensive way
> the sense in suffering, the method in the madness.
> God has chosen, instead, to remain hidden in mystery.[6]

Yes, God has chosen to remain a mystery. In his book *On First Principles*, first-century theologian Origen described what Paul meant when he wrote that God's judgments are "unsearchable" and His ways "unfathomable." Just read these words:

> Paul did not say that God's judgments were hard to
> search out but that they could not be searched out at
> all. He did not say that God's ways were hard to find

out but that they were impossible to find out. For however far one may advance in the search and make progress through an increasing earnest study, even when aided and enlightened in the mind by God's grace, he will never be able to reach the final goal of his inquiries.[7]

However, I believe strongly that it is not necessary for us to understand the hidden purposes of the Almighty in order to believe that such purposes exist. I also believe that someday we will be granted the ability to understand. "For now we see in a mirror dimly, but then face to face; now I know in part, but then I shall know fully just as I also have been fully known" (1 Corinthians 13:12, NASB). We see the jumbled bottom of the tapestry right now; only God sees the pattern from above.

The New Testament faces realistically the pain and evil of this world, but assures us that the future will make sense of the past. "I consider that our present sufferings are not worth comparing with the glory that will be revealed in us" (Romans 8:18). In the future, the unseen will give meaning to that which is seen. Eternity will interpret what happened in time. Meanwhile *we live by promises, not explanations*.

A Personal Answer

Where do we turn when the ambiguity of God's ways overwhelms us? Martin Luther, in pondering the mystery of

God's ways, urges us to "flee the hidden God and run to Christ." Now of course, the "hidden God" and the God who was made flesh are one and the same; they are not separate divinities between whom we must choose.

But as Stackhouse points out, it is precisely because the two are one that Luther's advice works. He writes, "One must run away from the mysteries of God's providence about which we cannot know enough to understand (because God has revealed so little about them), and run toward Jesus Christ in whom we find God adequately revealed."[8] Jesus assures us in His Word that He is for us and that nothing shall separate us from His love.

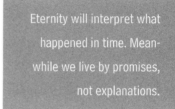

Eternity will interpret what happened in time. Meanwhile we live by promises, not explanations.

Look at the world and it might be hard to believe that God loves us and cares about us. At the very least, we could argue that God's attributes are ambiguous, at times caring, and at other times indifferent and callous. Based on a study of nature, we would not know whether God intended to punish us at the end of life or forgive us. Just read the history of philosophy and you will agree that no coherent idea of God can ever be formed on the basis of observation and experience.

If we want to discover whether God cares about His creation, we have to look beyond this world to His revelation. There we find hope that we could never discover on our own,

"For God so loved the world, that he gave his only begotten Son, that whosoever believeth in him should not perish, but have everlasting life" (John 3:16, KJV).

In his book *The Silence of God*, Sir Robert Anderson wrestles with the apparent indifference of God to human pain and tragedy. After asking all the important *why* questions, he writes the following passage, which deserves a careful reading:

> But of all the questions which immediately concern us, there is not one which the Cross of Christ has left unanswered. Men point to the sad incidents of human life on earth, and they ask, "Where is the love of God?" God points to that Cross as the unreserved manifestation of love so inconceivably infinite as to answer every challenge and silence all doubt forever. And that Cross is not merely the public proof of what God has accomplished; it is the earnest of all that He has promised. The crowning mystery of God is Christ, for in Him "are all the treasures of wisdom and knowledge hidden." And those hidden treasures are yet to be unfolded. It is the Divine purpose to "gather together in all things in Christ." *Sin has broken the harmony of creation, but that harmony shall yet be restored by the supremacy of our now despised and rejected Lord*[9] (italics added).

He says it was in the power of these truths that the martyrs died. Heaven was as silent then as it is now. Some reports say that when some Christian martyrs were marched to their death in France, they sang so loudly the authorities hired a band to drown out the sound of their hymns. No sights were seen, no voices heard, no deliverance granted. They looked in vain for some external proof that God was with them.

Speaking of similar martyrdoms, Anderson comments, "But with their spiritual vision focused upon Christ, the unseen realities of heaven filled their hearts, as they passed from a world that was not worthy of them to the home that God has prepared for them that love Him."[10] With their lives in jeopardy, they found comfort in Jesus.

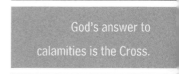

God's answer to calamities is the Cross.

Damaris Carbaugh sings:

> *Christ in me, the hope of glory*
> *Christ in me, the shelter from the storm*
> *Should men of evil have their day,*
> *Or should the earth's foundations sway,*
> *None of these can take away the living Christ in me.*

Words and music by Marie Armenia.
© Penny Hill Publishing.

In Jesus, the curse of nature and the curse of humanity were borne so that we might be free from the debilitating effects of sin. God's answer to calamities is the Cross. "Christ redeemed us from the curse of the law by becoming a curse for us, for it is written: 'Cursed is everyone who is hung on a tree' " (Galatians 3:13).

Coping with Doubt

In order to illustrate the demands of faith, I've paraphrased a parable told by Basil Mitchell:

> In a time of war in an occupied country, a member of the resistance meets a stranger one night who deeply impresses him. They spend the night together in conversation. The stranger affirms that he also is on the side of the resistance—indeed, he is in charge of it. He urges the young partisan to have faith in him— no matter what. The young man is impressed with the stranger and decides to believe in him.
>
> The next day he sees the stranger fight on the side of the resistance, and he says to his friends, "See, the stranger is on our side." The young soldier's faith is vindicated.
>
> But the following day the stranger is in the uniform of a policeman handing members of the resistance to the occupying power—to the enemy!
>
> The young man's friends murmur against him, insisting that the stranger could not be on their side, because he was seen helping the enemy. But the young

partisan is undeterred, believing in the stranger no matter what.

Sometimes he requests help from the stranger and receives it; sometimes he asks for help and does not receive it. In times of such discouragement he affirms, "The stranger knows best."

This ambiguous behavior on the part of the stranger causes the young man's friends to ridicule his faith saying, "If that's what you mean by being on our side, the sooner he goes over to the other side the better!" Now the young man faces a dilemma: Does he conclude that the stranger is not on his side after all, or does he go on believing, no matter what?[11]

We can learn two lessons from this parable. First, our continued belief is dependent on the meeting we have had with Christ. If, when we see Jesus, we see God close to us, God loving us, God forgiving our sin, then we will be able to keep believing even though we do not have a final answer to the question of suffering.

And so, the answer as to how much we believe depends on the extent of our friendship with the Stranger (Christ). The better we know Him, the more likely we are to keep trusting Him, even when His actions are confusing and it appears He is not on our side.

We will not judge His love for us by our circumstances but by His promises. "For I am convinced that neither death nor life, neither angels nor demons, neither the present nor the future, nor any powers, neither height nor depth, nor anything else in all creation, will be able to separate us from the love of God that is in Christ Jesus our Lord" (Romans 8:38-39). To quote Stackhouse once more, "We can respond properly to evil in our lives because *we know that God is all-good and all-powerful because we know Jesus*"[12] (italics added).

Those of us who have come to know the Stranger are apt to believe His words of hope and comfort. To His disciples who were about to be bereft of their leader, and who would later die for their faith, Jesus gave this assurance: "Do not let your hearts be troubled. Trust in God; trust also in me. In my Father's house are many rooms; if it were not so, I would have told you. I am going there to prepare a place for you. And if I go and prepare a place for you, I will come back and take you to be with me that you also may be where I am. You know the way to the place where I am going" (John 14:1-4).

> Evil of all kinds is a problem for which God's plan of salvation is the solution.

This leads me to a second lesson from the parable: Questions about the mystery of evil are not solved in this life but in the next. You'll recall that on some days it appeared as if the stranger was on the side of the enemy and the conflict dragged on without resolution. But remember that God has all of eternity to explain to us (if He should so desire) the mystery of His ways. "Therefore we do not lose heart. Though outwardly we are wasting away, yet inwardly we are being renewed day by day. For our light and momentary troubles are achieving for us an eternal glory that far outweighs them all. So we fix our eyes not on what is seen, but on what is unseen. For what is seen is temporary, but what is unseen is eternal" (2 Corinthians 4:16-18).

Evil of all kinds is a problem for which God's plan of salvation is the solution. Through the Incarnation, Jesus is a participant in our suffering, not a distant observer. God is not far from us, uncaring, unthinking, and disconnected. We have the confidence that God will eventually make right His fallen creation. We should not affirm God's control over nature divorced from God's final triumph over this world and over history itself. Both must be believed.

Yes, ultimately the strength of our faith will be dependent on the One in whom we have come to trust. And we can face the uncertainty and trials of life with optimism, helping others along the way. "We can . . . know Jesus, and in his embrace, we can in turn embrace the suffering world and offer it a sure hope."[13]

Why doesn't our heavenly Father care for us as a good earthly father would—responding to our requests and shielding us from the plagues of this fallen world? The answer is that our heavenly Father loves us *more* than our earthly father could possibly love us, but He has a different set of priorities. We value health, and so does our heavenly Father; but He values our faith even more. He delights in providing food for us, but

He delights even more when we trust Him—though we are hungry and even starving to death. And yes, He delights when we trust Him even when He seems to be absent when we need Him the most.

If I may quote C. S. Lewis once more as he imagines the lead demon Screwtape saying to the demonic underling Wormwood, "Do not be deceived, Wormwood. Our cause is never more in danger than when a human, no longer desiring, but still intending, to do our Enemy's will [God's will], looks round upon a universe from which every trace of Him seems to have vanished, and asks why he has been forsaken, and still obeys."[14]

Even without a trace of God in the world, the man still obeys! What if God wanted to set up a series of circumstances to prove that some people will go on trusting Him even in the midst of pain, and in the absence of clear explanations? What if our faith means so much to the Almighty that He is willing that we suffer if only to prove our devotion and love even when so much in the world counts against His love and care?

The children weeping on CNN after they've lost their parents in an earthquake—that is not the last chapter in the history of this world. Skeptics are unconvinced, but those of us who have met the Stranger are convinced that He both knows and cares. We are also convinced that the last chapters of the book He is writing will someday clarify the meaning of the earlier smudged paragraphs.

You might remember the story about a blotch of black

paint that was spilled randomly on a canvas. A creative artist decided to paint a beautiful landscape working the black paint into the picture. What appeared to be destructive became part of a larger, more perfect design. In the end, every injustice will be answered, suffering will be redeemed, and God's glory will be displayed.

After John the Baptist was thrown into prison, he began to have second thoughts as to whether or not Christ was the Messiah. For one thing, the Old Testament predicted that when the Messiah came, the prisoners would be freed (see Isaiah 61:1). John made the same error as those who believe God is obligated to heal us today: He misinterpreted the timing and application of some of God's promises.

As long as John sat in the dungeon, it seemed that Christ was reneging on the promises of Isaiah. And I'm sure he reflected on how unfair it was that he who had played such a vital part in Christ's earthly ministry should be so summarily punished for taking a righteous stand against Herod's sinful marriage. So John sent a delegation to Christ to pointedly ask: "Are you the Expected One, or shall we look for someone else?" (Matthew 11:3, NASB). He was polite, but he was hurting badly. Jesus had disappointed him.

In response, Jesus reminded John that miracles were being done and then added, "And blessed is he who does not take offense at Me" (v. 6, NASB). We could paraphrase, *blessed is the person who is not upset with the way I run My business.*

Blessed is the person who does not say, "After the suffering

I saw as a result of an earthquake, I will never believe in God again." Blessed is the person who does not say, "I am never going to trust God because He did not keep me from injustice and abuse."

Blessed is the person who understands that we must trust God's heart when we cannot understand His hand; blessed is the person who knows that we must stand in awe in the presence of the mystery of God's purposes. Blessed is the person who keeps on believing no matter what. Blessed is the person who lets God be God.

Remember, birds sing not because they understand, but because they have a song.

QUESTIONS FOR DISCUSSION

1. Do you believe that God is worthy of our trust? Why or why not?

2. What would you do if you had God's powers—and wisdom—for twenty-four hours?

3. Are there times when you have doubted either the existence or goodness of God? Discuss.

4. Why is it that when life seems most unstable, people often turn to God for comfort?

CHAPTER 6

WHAT DO YOU SAY WHEN FRIENDS ASK?

What do we say when our friends ask about God's role in natural disasters? Some ask because they are seekers, weighing the merits of the Christian faith. Others are believers, but the magnitude of horrific suffering makes them wonder where God was, or whether He cares.

Let's begin by pointing out that we all are asking the same questions, and we do not have a list of ready answers, slickly packaged and ready for distribution. Intuitively, we know there are no pat answers or glib comments that will advance the dialogue or convince the mind. Yet, speak we must.

So, what *do* you say?

We Must Grieve

We must begin any discussion of tragedy by grieving for those who are in pain. Many of us are better at trying to explain natural disasters than we are at weeping over them! An entire book of the Old Testament describes in vivid detail the grief that the prophet Jeremiah experienced after the devastation of Jerusalem. No doubt most of the people were disobedient, disregarding God's warnings. But it's likely that many God-fearing people were also killed or starved to death in the siege. Jeremiah recognized that even when the cruel Babylonians came, God was in charge; it was God who inflicted the judgment, but the prophet still wept, just as we should.

Jeremiah writes as though the city herself is speaking:

> Is it nothing to you, all you who pass by? Look around and see. Is any suffering like my suffering that was inflicted on me, that the LORD brought upon me in the day of his fierce anger? From on high he sent fire, sent it down into my bones. He spread a net for my feet and turned me back. He made me desolate, faint all the day long. . . .
>
> This is why I weep and my eyes overflow with tears. No one is near to comfort me, no one to restore my spirit. My children are destitute because the enemy has prevailed.
>
> **LAMENTATIONS 1:12-13, 16**

Jeremiah models for us a blending of human compassion and solid theology. Yes, *God* brought judgment upon the people by using evil people to destroy Jerusalem. But the prophet is not angry with the Almighty, nor does he stoically accept suffering because it was deserved. He grieves over the ruined city. He laments the fact that the people were so disobedient that they invited punishment.

Natural disasters cause us to pause, they cause us to ask hard questions, and if we care about the world, they drive us to tears. Can anyone staring at the destruction caused by the tsunami not weep? Surely a heart of human compassion identifies with the loss, the suffering, and the hopelessness of fellow human beings. We should not approach disasters with an accusatory finger or a detached attitude. Grieving hearts can only be touched by other grieving hearts—sharing pain and mingling tears.

Any answer must begin with personal compassion and a heavy heart.

Tears, if they are not wasted, should lead to deeds. The church is called to suffer and to die with the world and nowhere is that more necessary than where tragedy strikes. Some believers suffer because they are caught in the tragedy itself; others suffer because they are willing to sacrifice for others. I commend those who are willing to leave the comforts of home in order to bring hope and healing

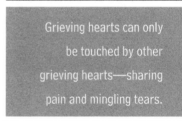

Grieving hearts can only be touched by other grieving hearts—sharing pain and mingling tears.

to the victims. Not everyone can go, but we can all give; we can all participate in helping relief agencies as they serve those who are so utterly destitute. When disaster strikes, the church should be the church!

As she surveyed the repairs done on her home by relief workers, one survivor of Hurricane Katrina commented, "If it weren't for the Christians, we would have no hope here in the Gulf Coast. We needed them, and they showed up." What better witness to the hurting people in this world than to minister to their physical needs first? God wants us to release our grip on our money, our resources, and our selfishness. When disasters come, we should be the first to respond with sacrifice and generosity.

We begin with grief, and then we seek for understanding.

We Must Give Thanks

We must remember that natural disasters are an intensification of what is happening every day in our world—people are dying of starvation, storms, and disease. The fact that we are alive is a reminder of God's goodness. We are living on a cursed earth and death will take us all at one time or another. Thanks to sin, this planet is not a safe place.

Natural disasters should remind us of all of the blessings we take for granted; they should lead us to deep and lasting gratitude. Before we ask why so many die in natural disasters, we should ask a different question: "Why are so many people—ourselves included—*still living*?" We've learned that sunshine and crops are a sign of God's mercy, and that disasters reflect His justice and yes, even anger. Yet how many

> Before we ask why so many die in natural disasters, we should ask a different question: "Why are so many people—ourselves included—still living?"

people give Him thanks for beautiful weather and the numerous benefits that nature regularly bestows upon this planet?

Every day that we live with sunshine, food, and health, we are enjoying gifts God does not have to give us. He multiplies blessings for both the righteous and the unrighteous: "But I tell you: Love your enemies and pray for those who persecute you, that you may be sons of your Father in heaven. *He causes his sun to rise on the evil and the good, and sends rain on the righteous and the unrighteous*" (Matthew 5:44-45, italics added).

And so the sun shines to warm us, the rain falls to bless us, and the stars shine to remind us that God is not only in heaven, but also on earth to give us mercies we do not deserve. We should be grateful for the times when the earth is firm, when the tornadoes do not blow, and when the floods do not come. The same book of Lamentations that describes the grief of Jeremiah says, "Because of the LORD's great love we are not consumed, for his compassions never fail. They are new every morning; great is your faithfulness" (Lamentations 3:22-23).

Life is a gift and God has the right to give it and take it. We cannot approach this question with an attitude of entitlement, believing that we have the right to life, liberty, and happiness. We can pursue these things, but thanks to our sins and those of our forefathers, God is not obligated to give us the blessings He graciously chooses to send our way.

Often the same people who ask where God was following a disaster thanklessly refuse to worship and honor Him for years of peace and calmness. They disregard God in good times, yet think He is obligated to provide help when bad times come. They believe the God they dishonor when they are well should heal them when they are sick; the God they ignore when they are wealthy should rescue them from impending poverty; and the God they refuse to worship when the earth is still should rescue them when it begins to shake.

> Natural disasters force us to decide how we will respond to God.

We must admit that God owes us nothing. Before we charge God with not caring, we must thank Him for those times when His care is very evident. We are ever surrounded by undeserved blessings. Even in His silence, He blesses us.

We Must Choose

Let's tell our friends that natural disasters force us to decide how we will respond to God. We can either become angry or we can choose to stand in awe of the Almighty. We can accuse Him or we can worship Him, but neutrality will be difficult, if not impossible.

That is the dilemma that Job faced when his children died in a windstorm. When news reached him of the lightning and the high winds, he did not know the prologue to his book. He did not know that Satan and God had had a dialogue and that he had been singled out for a special trial. Without explanation, without knowing the fine print of God's purposes, lightning killed all of Job's cattle and a windstorm (likely a tornado) killed his children.

Satan told God that if Job had his possessions taken from him, he would "curse" God to His face (Job 1:11). Interestingly, scholars tell us that the word *barak* in Hebrew can mean either bless or curse, depending on the context. Although his wife, overcome with sorrow, encouraged Job to turn against God—"curse God and die" (Job 2:9)—Job would have no part of it. With the keen insight of a theologian, he corrected her. "Shall we accept good from God, and not trouble?" (Job 2:10). He knew that both the shining sun and the powerful lightning came from God.

With ten fresh graves on the side of a hill, Job chose to *bless* and not *curse*. In response to God, he worshipped:

> Naked I came from my mother's womb, and naked I will depart. The LORD gave and the LORD has taken away; may the name of the LORD be praised.   **JOB 1:21**

The next day, things went from bad to worse. By now Satan had permission from God to smite Job with "painful sores from the soles of his feet to the top of his head" (Job 2:7). Again, Job had to choose: Should he worship God or curse Him? Again he chose the path of worship and proved *it is possible to worship God without explanations.*

Natural disasters might drive some people away from God, but for others it has the opposite effect, driving them into the arms of Jesus. The destruction of nature has helped them distinguish the temporary from the permanent. Disasters remind the living that tomorrow is uncertain, so we must prepare for eternity today. Today is the accepted time; today is the day of salvation.

When disasters come, God is not on trial, *we are*.

We Must Find Firm Ground

Finally, we come to the one clear lesson that natural disasters teach us: Even the things that appear solid will someday quake beneath our feet. We must remind our friends to find firm ground while they can.

One day I spoke to a man who survived an earthquake. He said that those ten seconds seemed like an eternity because he did not know when they would end and where he would be when it was over. He ran out onto the street because he could not trust his house to withstand the shock. In that moment, what he wanted more than anything was firm ground.

The Bible instructs us to make sure that our lives are built upon a foundation that will never be shaken, a foundation that is not subject to the unpredictable forces of nature. The upheavals of nature pry us loose from faith in everything transitory, everything that will eventually be destroyed. Earthquakes and the tsunamis they sometimes generate are the voice of God shouting to an unrepentant planet.

The first recorded earthquake in the Bible occurred when God gave the law at Mount Sinai. Let's put ourselves in the trembling sandals of the Israelites.

> Mount Sinai was covered with smoke, because the LORD descended on it in fire. The smoke billowed up from it like smoke from a furnace, the whole mountain trembled violently, and the sound of the trumpet grew louder and louder. Then Moses spoke and the voice of God answered him.
>
> **EXODUS 19:18-19**

I believe the mountain trembled because God wanted the people to stand in awe of His power and be appropriately afraid to approach Him carelessly. The voice of words spelled out the content of the moral law; the voice of nature spelled out His power and authority. The Ten Commandments shouted His rules for living; the trembling of nature shouted His rules for worshipping. To fear Him was not only appropriate, but commanded.

Now let's skip the centuries and consider the earthquake that coincided with Jesus' death. "At that moment the curtain of the temple was torn in two from top to bottom. The earth shook and the rocks split" (Matthew 27:51).

The timing of the earthquake at Sinai and the earthquake

> Natural disasters teach us that even the things that appear solid will someday quake beneath our feet.

at Calvary could not have been more precise. Two earth-quakes, two acts of revelation, and two judgments. On Mount Sinai God spoke the law with its inflexible demands and warned of the consequences of disobedience; on Calvary God spoke words of kindness and mercy through the lips of Jesus, even while He was judged for our sins. Both events were accompanied by the shaking of the earth, a reminder that when God speaks, the mountains and rocks tremble.

> In the final judgment, the whole earth will be destroyed and be recreated by God.

These two events are given an interesting interpretation in the book of Hebrews. The writer makes a contrast between the old covenant where God shook the earth at Sinai, and the new covenant that was instituted at Calvary. In this new covenant, God is seen as speaking from heaven. Let's let the author describe it:

> See to it that you do not refuse him who speaks. If they did not escape when they refused him who warned them on earth, how much less will we, if we turn away from him who warns us from heaven? At that time his voice shook the earth, but now he has promised, "Once more I will shake not only the earth but also the heavens." The words "once more" indicate the removing of what can be shaken—that is, created things—so that what cannot be shaken may remain.
>
> **HEBREWS 12:25-27**

There are three "shakings" of the earth mentioned here. The first was at Sinai, the second was at Calvary, and the third is yet to come. The worst natural disaster of all time is still in the future! Everything that can be shaken will be shaken so that only the unshakable will remain.

And now the conclusion:

> Therefore, since we are receiving a kingdom that cannot be shaken, let us be thankful, and so worship God acceptably with reverence and awe, **for our "God is a consuming fire."**
>
> **HEBREWS 12:28-29 (emphasis added)**

The final natural disaster will split the world into two separate kingdoms: the unshakable Kingdom of God and the disintegrating kingdom of the damned.

Natural disasters shake not just the earth, but also our confidence that the earth will go on forever, and that our own place in the world is predictable and within our power. Just because natural law appears uniform, we cannot retain our own independence from God and His purposes indefinitely.

Earthquakes and hurricanes vividly remind us that life is short, and the triumph of God over this world is certain. There is a time coming when everything that has been nailed down will be torn up. And in the final judgment, the whole earth will be destroyed and recreated by God. Then, only what is eternal will remain. Tragedies teach us to hold onto Christ tightly and everything else loosely.

Yes, natural disasters are God's megaphone, shouting to this world. But that is not the only way God speaks to us. You may recall that Elijah the prophet was asked to go stand on a mountain in the presence of the Lord as the Almighty passed by. We read:

> Then a great and powerful wind tore the mountains apart and shattered the rocks before the LORD, but the LORD was not in the wind. After the wind there was an earthquake, but the LORD was not in the earthquake. After the earthquake came a fire, but the LORD was not in the fire. **And after the fire came a gentle whisper.**
>
> **1 KINGS 19:11-12 (emphasis added)**

Sometimes God shouts and sometimes He whispers. If we are quiet, we can hear His voice asking us to turn from our own self-absorption to Him. To turn from the uncertainties of this life to the certainty of the next. To exchange our own petty kingdoms for one that will endure.

If He will not be heard in natural disasters, perhaps God will be heard in the quietness of our souls. Perhaps we will take the time to ponder His mercy and heed the warnings He has given, through Jesus Christ our Lord.

> Therefore keep watch, because you do not know on what day your Lord will come. But understand this: If the owner of the house had known at what time of night the thief was coming,

he would have kept watch and would not have let his house
be broken into. So you also must be ready, because the Son of
Man will come at an hour when you do not expect him.

MATTHEW 24:42-44

Blessed are those who realize the uncertainties of this life
are a reminder to prepare for the certainties to come.

"Worship God acceptably with reverence and awe, for our
'God is a consuming fire' " (Hebrews 12:28-29).

QUESTIONS FOR DISCUSSION

1. Where do you find firm ground when the world around you
   seems shaken to the core?

2. What do you say to friends who wonder about God's role in natural disasters?

3. When disaster strikes, is your first inclination to bless or curse
   God? Why?

READY FOR THE BIG ONE

Almost every time I visit California someone is talking about earthquakes, and many residents are expecting "the big one" that could destroy most of Los Angeles and the surrounding areas. For years, geologists have known that the San Andreas fault, which runs near the coast, is vulnerable to a massive earthquake that could dwarf all others experienced so far.

But the really "big one" will not be confined to California; it will encompass the whole earth. When Christ comes to wrap up history as we know it, the earth and everything in it will be destroyed. This earth, cursed as it is by sin, will burn with fire, and God will remake it according to His specifications.

In the last chapter we discussed the shaking of the earth, but another passage in the New Testament says the universe itself will disappear, destroyed in a giant inferno. Nothing we have ever seen will compare with it:

> But the day of the Lord will come like a thief. The heavens will disappear with a roar; the elements will be destroyed by fire,

and the earth and everything in it will be laid bare. Since everything will be destroyed in this way, what kind of people ought you to be? You ought to live holy and godly lives as you look forward to the day of God and speed its coming. That day will bring about the destruction of the heavens by fire, and the elements will melt in the heat. But in keeping with his promise we are looking forward to a new heaven and a new earth, the home of righteousness.   **2 PETER 3:10-13**

The conclusion follows:

So then, dear friends, since you are looking forward to this, make every effort to be found spotless, blameless and at peace with him.   **2 PETER 3:14**

In the final destruction of the cosmos, all that will remain is God, the devil, angels, and people. Quite a reminder of what is really important! Of course, the present earth will be recreated and eternity will officially begin (see Revelation 21:1).

The question before us is simple: How do we escape the penalty meted out at the final judgment? It makes little difference whether we are alive when Christ comes or whether we die and He returns decades later. In one way or another we will all participate in the end-time scenario. Attendance at the final judgment is mandatory.

If you are wise, you will be prepared for the "big one."

Avoiding the Final Curse

Here is the good news: This world is in trouble, but Jesus came to rescue us from its final consequences. "But the Scripture declares that the whole world is a prisoner of sin, so that what was promised, being given through faith in Jesus Christ, might be given to those who believe" (Galatians 3:22).

The whole world is a prisoner of sin! What a vivid description of our planet, with its suffering, sin, and death. But Jesus came to remove the curse for those who believe in Him. Let me quote this verse once more: "Christ redeemed us from the curse of the law by becoming a curse for us, for it is written: 'Cursed is everyone who is hung on a tree.' He redeemed us in order that the blessing given to Abraham might come to the Gentiles through Christ Jesus, so that by faith we might receive the promise of the Spirit" (Galatians 3:13-14).

> In one way or another we will all participate in the end-time scenario. Attendance at the final judgment is mandatory.

Jesus bore the last judgment for all who believe in Him. When we receive Him as our sin-bearer we are given the gift of His righteousness so that we can be welcomed into God's presence as if we had never sinned. But only Jesus is qualified to prepare us for eternity because He was not just a teacher, but a *Savior.*

Back in the days when homesteaders were on the prairies, they would frequently light a fire around their homes at a time when the wind was favorable. They knew that prairie fires could begin in the distance and a fierce wind could blow the flames toward them. But when they burned the grass and weeds around their homes, they knew they were safe because *they were living where the fire had already been.*

Just so, when we transfer our trust to Jesus, we are standing where the fire of God's judgment has already come. "Whoever believes in the Son has eternal life, but whoever rejects the Son will not see life, for God's wrath remains on him" (John 3:36). As we learned in the last chapter, our God is a consuming fire.

> Only Jesus is qualified to prepare us for eternity because He was not just a teacher, but a Savior.

Missouri pastor Keith Simon, in a message to his congregation, said, "Christ did not come to this world to suffer massive shame and pain because Americans are pretty good people. The magnitude of Christ's suffering is owing to how deeply we deserve Katrina—all of us."[1] In Jesus, we learn that God is not distant and remote when we suffer. In Jesus, God suffered that He might redeem us from the final suffering of hell.

We all remember the images of the refugees surrounding the Superdome in New Orleans, preparing for their bus trip to various other cities. Some politicians objected to the word *refugee*, insisting that they simply be called evacuees. Regardless, these people are a metaphor of our own lives. We, too, are searching for a new beginning, without water and food. We are all trekking as best we can, en route to our final destination. What we need is a refuge, somewhere that is safe, somewhere that guarantees us a future with God in heaven.

The sons of Korah invite us to run to God for safety when the earth begins to shake. They knew that *God is the only refuge for refugees*.

> God is our refuge and strength, an ever-present help in trouble. Therefore we will not fear, though the earth give way and the mountains fall into the heart of the sea, though its waters roar and foam and the mountains quake with their surging.
>
> There is a river whose streams make glad the city of God, the holy place where the Most High dwells.
>
> God is within her, she will not fall; God will help her at break of day. Nations are in an uproar, kingdoms fall; he lifts his voice, the earth melts. The LORD Almighty is with us; the God of Jacob is our fortress.
>
> Come and see the works of the LORD, the desolations he has brought on the earth. He makes wars cease to the ends of the earth; he breaks the bow and shatters the spear, he burns the shields with fire.
>
> Be still, and know that I am God; I will be exalted among the nations, I will be exalted in the earth. The LORD Almighty is with us; the God of Jacob is our fortress. **PSALM 46**

A Prayer

Father in heaven, I confess the mystery of Your ways. I do not understand Your long-term agenda, nor can I fathom the hidden purposes You have in the pain of the people You created. Yet I do know that I am a sinner, judged in many different ways for my sin. But I thank You that Jesus died to remove the curse, to free me from Your righteous anger about my rebellion. So in this moment, I receive Jesus as my sinbearer, as the One who died in my place. I affirm this promise for myself: "Yet to all who received him, to those who believed in his name, he gave the right to become children of God—children born not of natural descent, nor of human decision or a husband's will, but born of God" (John 1:12-13).

Thank you for receiving me, for I pray in Jesus' name, Amen.

INTRODUCTION

1 Fyodor Dostoyevsky, Constance Garnett, trans., *The Brothers Karamazov,* Modern Library Series (New York: Random House, 1995), 272.

CHAPTER 1

1 Susan Neiman, *Evil in Modern Thought* (Princeton: Princeton University Press, 2002), 142.

2 A. J. Conyers, *The Eclipse of Heaven* (Downers Grove: InterVarsity Press, 1992), 13.

3 Ibid., 13. Quotation is from Kendrick, *The Lisbon Earthquake* (Philadelphia: Lippincott, 1957), 137.

4 Conyers, *The Eclipse of Heaven*, 13.

5 John Woodbridge, ed., *Great Leaders of the Christian Church* (Chicago: Moody Press, 1988), 174.

6 Joseph McCabe, ed. and trans., *Selected Works of Voltaire* (London: Watts and Co., 1911), at http://courses.essex.ac.uk/cs/cs101/VOLT/Lisbon2.htmlast accessed 5/2/06.

7 http://humanities.uchicago.edu/homes/VSA/letters/24.11.1755.html; last accessed 3/24/06.

8 Voltaire, *Candide* (New York: New American Library, 1961), 26.

9 Ibid., 28.

10 William Barclay, *The Letter to the Romans* (Edinburgh: The Saint Andrew Press, 1955), 115.

11 Edward Rothstein, "Seeking Justice, of Gods or the Politicians," *The New York Times* (September 8, 2005).

12 David B. Hart, "Tremors of Doubt," *OpinionJournal* (December 31, 2004), at http://www.opinionjournal.com/taste/?id=110006097; last accessed 4/19/06.

CHAPTER 2

1 http://www.usatoday.com/weather/tornado/storms/1999/w503tor0.htm last accessed 5/2/06.

2 "The Lost and Helpless Flee from Hell to the Hills," *Independent Foreign News* (August 26, 1999).

3 Tony Campolo, "Katrina: Not God's Wrath—or His Will," www.Beliefnet.com (January 8, 2006).

4 For an in-depth critique of Openness Theology, consult Bruce Ware, *God's Lesser Glory* (Wheaton, IL: Crossway Publishing, 2000).

5 John Stuart Mill, *Nature: The Utility of Religion and Theism* (Watts & Co., The Rationalist Press, 1904), 21.

6 John Piper, "Whence and Why?" *World Magazine* (September 4, 1999), 33.

7 Timothy Lull, ed., *Martin Luther's Basic Theological Writings* (Minneapolis: Augsburg Fortress Publishers, 1989), 744.

8 Ibid., 742.

9 William Cowper, "God Moves In a Mysterious Way," *Cowper's Poems,* Hugh I'Anson, ed. (New York: Everyman's Library, 1966), 188-189.

10 Quoted in Charles Swindoll, *The Mystery of God's Will* (Nashville: W Publishing Group, 1999), 115.

CHAPTER 3

1 Kim Barker, "Many Faithful Spared When Mass Relocated," *Chicago Tribune* (January 5, 2005), sec. 1, 6.

2 Bill Hekman, pastor of Calvary Life Fellowship in Indonesia (February 22, 2005), America Online: Learylegal.

3 Amy Waldman, "Faith Divides the Survivors and It Unites Them Too," www2.kenyon.edu/Depts/Religion/Fac/Adler/Misc/Tsunami-survivors.htm last accessed 3/27/06.

4 Max Lucado, "What Katrina Can Teach Us," *Pulpit Helps*, vol. 30, no. 11 (November 2005), 5.

5 James Houston, ed., *The Mind on Fire—An Anthology of the Writings of Blaise Pascal* (Portland: Multnomah Press, 1989), 51.

6 Ibid., 51.

7 Jill Lawrence, *USA Today,* "Behind an Iconic Photo, One Family's Tale of Grief" (November 11–13, 2005), 1, 6A.

8 David Miller, "God and Katrina," http://www.apologeticspress.org/articles/351.

9 C. S. Lewis, *Paved with Good Intentions* (New York: HarperCollins, 2005), 24.

10 Ibid., 25.

CHAPTER 4

1 Brett Martel, "Angry God Sent Storms, Mayor of New Orleans Says," *Chicago Tribune* (January 17, 2006), sec. 1, 6.

2 Dennis Behrendt, "Why Does God Allow Calamities?" *The New American* (December 26, 2005), 32.

3 Michael Luo, "Doomsday: The Latest Word If Not the Last," *New York Times* (October 16, 2005).

4 *World Magazine*, "Letters to the Editor" (September–October 2005).

5 Byron Paulus, *Revival Report*, Life Action Ministries (Fall 2005), 2.

6 "New Orleans City Council President: 'Maybe God's Going To Cleanse Us," LifeSiteNews.com (September, 1, 2005).

7 http://www.spiritdaily.org/New-world-order/neworleans.htm; last accessed 5/2/06.

8 As quoted in *AgapePress,* "God's Mercy Evident in Katrina's Wake" (September 2, 2005).

9 Paulus, *Revival Report*, 3.

CHAPTER 5

1 C. S. Lewis, *Mere Christianity* (New York: HarperCollins, 1952), 38.

2 Ibid., 29.

3 Ravi Zacharias, "The Silence of Christmas and the Scream of the Tsunami," *Just Thinking* (Winter 2005), 1.

4 As quoted in the editorial, "Tsunamis and Birth Pangs," *Christianity Today* (February 2005), 28.

5 I'm indebted to J. M. Monsabre for this idea, as quoted in *12,000 Religious Quotations*, Frank Mead, ed. (Grand Rapids: Baker Book House, 1989), 179.

6 John Stackhouse, *Can God Be Trusted?—Faith and the Challenge of Evil* (New York: Oxford University Press, 1988), 103.

7 Origen, *On First Principles* (New York: Harper and Row, 1966).

8 Stackhouse, *Can God Be Trusted?* 103.

9 Sir Robert Anderson, *The Silence of God* (Grand Rapids: Kregel Publications, 1952), 150–151.

10 Ibid., 152.

11 http://72.14.207.104/search?q=cache:t5Sc3AWQXrcJ:tre.ngfl.gov.uk/ uploads/materials/14455/ gardener1.pdf+basil+mitchell+stranger+knows+best&hl=en&gl=us&ct =clnk&cd=3; last accessed 5/2/06.

12 Stackhouse, *Can God Be Trusted?* 104.

13 As quoted in the editorial, "Tsunamis and Birth Pangs," *Christianity Today* (February 2005), 28. Found at http://www.christianitytoday.com/ct/2005/002/4.28.html; last accessed 4/25/06.

14 C. S. Lewis, *Paved with Good Intentions* (New York: HarperCollins, 2005), 38.

EPILOGUE
1 http://www.dirpodcast.com/podcasts/index.php?iid=1211; last accessed 5/2/06.

FREE DISCUSSION QUESTIONS INCLUDED!

A reproducible version of this
book's discussion questions is available at:

ChristianBookGuides.com

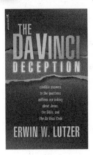
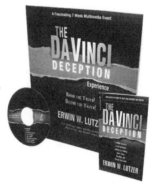
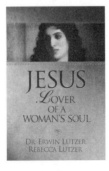